Introducing the Lessons of the Church Year

A Guide for Lay Readers and Congregations

FREDERICK HOUK BORSCH

TRINITY PRESS INTERNATIONAL · PHILADELPHIA

First Trinity Press International Edition 1991

Trinity Press International
P.O. Box 851
Valley Forge, PA 19482-0851

Cover design by Jim Gerhard

Library of Congress Cataloging-in-Publication Data

Borsch, Frederick Houk.
    Introducing the lessons of the church year : a guide for lay
readers and congregations / Frederick Houk Borsch. — 1st Trinity
Press ed.
      p. cm.
    Originally published: New York : Seabury Press, 1978.
    Includes bibliographical references and index.
    ISBN 1-56338-025-0
    1. Bible—Liturgical lessons, English. 2. Reading in public
worship. 3. Episcopal Church—Liturgy. 4. Anglican Communion—
Liturgy. I. Title.
BS391.2.B67   1991
264'.03034—dc20   91-24924
                                           CIP
93 94 95 96 97 98 99   6 5 4 3 2

Printed in the United States of America

Contents

Foreword

This book has been prepared to help those who know something about the Bible be of assistance to those who have relatively little such understanding. It is written in the belief that even a small amount of guidance can spark considerable interest in the biblical stories, and that the poems, parables, and prophesies of the scriptures will then provide their own fuel. Although the book can be used without reference to the opening chapters, they are provided as counsel to lay readers and others who may have questions about the role of the Bible in worship and find benefit in basic advice with regard to reading in public.

The lectionary schedule which is followed is that of the *Book of Common Prayer* of the Episcopal Church. Many of these readings are also designated by other churches for use on the same Sundays or major holidays. Where there is variation in another church's lectionary, the appropriate introduction can often be found by consulting the Index of Biblical Readings in order to locate the page where an introduction to the different reading is given.

It pleases me to see *Introducing the Lessons of the Church Year* in this new edition. It was published first by Seabury Press, then by Winston Press, and finally by Harper and Row. I have enjoyed seeing and hearing it used, noticing it in many church sacristies, knowing that it has been given to new readers and used in classes for them, and receiving letters of appreciation and suggestions. It was good to learn, for example, that a number of people found the "Index of Biblical Readings" valuable as it enabled them to see when particular passages occur during the three cycles of the liturgical year. I have sought to incorporate a number of the suggestions sent to me, make certain other revisions, and to bring the lists of suggested readings and of the versions of the Bible up-to-date.

I wish to thank again the colleagues and congregations who helped with the writing of the first edition, and also Louis Weil, O. C. Edwards, John Koenig, Joseph Russell, Peter Carlson, Laura Barrett, and Harold Rast who have offered assistance for this edition.

The Uses of the Introductions

Many who attend church do not hear the Bible as it is read to them. Even the casual observer on a Sunday morning notices the wandering eyes and blank expressions. From the lectern there may pour down hot words of judgment followed by the comic twists of one of Jesus' parables. Empty faces betray nary a flicker of emotion. (One is, of course, entitled to ask this observer how well he himself is listening while making these notations. I remind myself of the man who accused his pastor of gazing about the church during the general confession.)

There are no magic formulas which will change this situation. Although we will soon make a strong argument for the liturgical reading of the scriptures, people cannot be forced to listen carefully to stories and prophecies which are in several ways foreign to their experience. Thoughtful hearing of the Bible requires study and reflection along with a personal readiness to involve the will and imagination. Brief introductions will not make up for a lack of instruction, discussion and interpretive preaching.

Yet there are ways to help, and this book is written in the conviction that many individuals want to pay closer attention to readings from the Bible. I also believe that they are quite capable of reflective listening if they are given only a little assistance.

The introductions offered here are meant to sharpen hearing. They are, for the most part, summaries of the readings—drawing out major themes. While interpretation is inevitable and some additional information and comment are consciously presented, their main purpose is to prepare those ready to listen for what they are about to hear. It is difficult—even for those trained in the study of the Bible—to find oneself suddenly in the midst of a passage from Deuteronomy, one of the prophets, or a letter of Paul. Told, however, that I am about to hear the account of a vision in which the prophet foresees the Lord bringing the people of God home from exile, I may well be able to share something of the experience.

One way of employing the introductions would be to place them in the Sunday bulletins. They have been written so that the opening sentence (printed here in bold type) could be used by itself, or the longer statement might be included.

Those who read the scriptures aloud might preface the lessons with the first sentence or some other form of the introductions in this book. The longer versions in their entirety would likely provide too much verbalization for most congregational settings.

Readers may wish to use these introductions as guides for prefaces of their own composing, oriented to the needs of a particular congregation. The introductions offered here are, for instance, somewhat formal in style. A different form might be felt suitable for certain situations.

A word of caution, however: without careful planning it is easy to slip over from a brief focusing statement into a little sermon. A sermon or homily has its important place in liturgy, but it is customary that there be no more than one for each service and that the scriptures be heard first before they are expounded. I see the primary function of the introductions in helping listeners to hear, not telling them how to hear.

Another possible use of these introductions is for private reflection before reading or listening to the lessons in church. Although obviously no substitute for the scriptures, the prefaces may help to provide insight and overall comprehension. In similar ways groups engaged in Bible study might find guidance from the introductions. Other groups could use the book to find biblical passages they wish to study or which may be appropriate to the theme of a particular meeting or conference.

I know that I have discovered all kinds of new understandings by working through these passages, not only Sunday by Sunday in a single cycle, but also by reviewing all the lessons for a particular day from the three cycles. Readers may find it an aid for their own meditations to contemplate the many themes set out in all the introductions for, as an example, Trinity Sunday while reflecting on God's love and presence as Creator, Redeemer and sanctifying Spirit.

It may be helpful to add a few words concerning the composition of these introductions. I did not follow the same procedures in every case, but it was customary to study the passage in the several translations which are most likely to be used for public reading (see pages 15–17) and in the original languages. I often found it beneficial to consult commentaries, especially for opinions on disputed and difficult passages. My goal was to try to discover what the reading was first intended to mean before reflecting on some of its implications for contemporary people. I then attempted to state the essential themes or events of the lesson, beginning with a comprehensive sentence. Frequently it seemed helpful to add a word or phrase with reference to material not actually found in the reading but which seemed to set it in its immediate context or the wider context of, for instance, Paul's ministry or Jesus' teaching. Indeed, sometimes it might have been misleading if this were not done. In many cases it seemed unnecessary to add further guidance. With other lessons, however, a few brief hints or suggestions at ways of interpretation and involving oneself in the materials appeared to be called for. I hope that this has not been done in such a way as to dictate the understanding of the passage, but rather to provide illumination for the reader and listener.

I found dangers all around, and I am certain not all have been escaped. Often I discovered that one of my introductions was so compactly written that it had to be rethought and clarified. Of even greater concern was the tendency while summarizing to make unwarranted generalizations, or to omit or juxtapose ideas in such a way as to make the lesson say something other than it does. One of the hardest problems faced was dealing with passages containing verses which have been interpreted and sometimes translated in strikingly different ways. In some instances I have been able to indicate this difficulty. More often a decision had to be made about the meaning, although, wherever possible, I wrote with the intention of leaving such a passage open to different understandings.

I attempted to keep the season of the church year in mind and to be aware of interrelationships within the lessons. At the same time, I wanted the individual passages to be heard for themselves and frequently found it unnecessary to stress the obvious. I also reminded myself that all three lessons, together with the psalm, would not be used in every service, and that the introductions should not, therefore, be written in such a way as to require one another for their understanding.

Why We Read the Bible in Church

Making Community

People find an identity and gain a sense of sharing together through the stories they have in common. We recognize this to be true in all manner of circumstances. Former college roommates come together and reestablish community by rehearsing tales of late night escapades and courses flunked or passed together. "Do you remember the look on old Professor Donner's face. . . .?" "When Louise came back and found Hank asleep in the middle of the floor. . . ."

Probably nowhere is the significance of common stories more evident than in the family. Around the dinner table, during holiday seasons, before and after funerals, the family narratives are recounted. Of course, in many cases there is no need to retell them in their entirety. A few words of reference to a particular object may be enough to reawaken memories. In my parents' home an awkwardly repaired lamp is a kind of symbol for a whole series of events involving a too-adventurous, sometimes deceitful son and his forgiving parents.

There are times when the family will want to trace its roots down even farther—to sayings or anecdotes about ancestors long dead. Perhaps a scrap of foreign language is remembered along with the story through several generations. "When great grandmother lost her temper, they say she went around shouting, 'bei Gott im Himmel' at everyone in sight including the dog and cat." There may well be stories about a famous relative who acted heroically and with whom all can proudly identify.

Such narratives provide threads of continuity. By means of the story a texture of order and belonging is woven. The drifting and tumbled character of life is given a measure of design and some sense of meaning.

We know that narratives are also vital for larger communities—for a city or region, especially for a nation or ethnic group. Collections of stories, sayings, legends and songs help tell them who they are. To be a member of the community is to know these materials.

They will be taught in the schools or in other community institutions. Customs and symbols arise out of the stories, and strangers can be immediately recognized by their failure to perceive the significance of them. Not to have such experiences in common with some group of people is, sadly, not to belong anywhere.

One can speak of the Bible as the common or community lore of Christianity. Christians may journey to distant locales and meet with disciples of widely diverse cultures and lifestyles. By means of books and works of art they may *travel* in history and encounter the experiences and reflections of Christian men and women from far-away eras and societies. Even in their own city or town there are usually opportunities to converse with Christians representing different age-groups and denominational or ethnic backgrounds. They will worship and reflect their faith in different ways: Pentecostalists and Quakers, Shakers and Catholics. Varying levels of education and social and economic circumstances can also affect the language of faith. Searching disciples reading the works of different theologians may be struck by the disparity in their idiom or accent as they talk about Christianity.

There is, however, one communal feature in the experience of all these Christians. They have, as it were, a common language. To the extent that they have become full members of the community they share a body of sayings, stories and symbols which are the fundamental lore of Christianity. From the Bible—and especially the Gospels—Christians of different centuries, classes and countries draw upon the same stock of adventures, prophecies, songs, commandments, visions and parables. Wherever one goes there is found among Christians this bond and therefore this sense of community: the remembrance of exodus and exile, of Moses and David, Jeremiah and Jonah, the narrative of a child's humble birth, of shared meals, the bread and wine, the cross, and the vibrant new hope which followed—on the road to Emmaus and the road to Damascus.

From the beginning these experiences and the stories which molded the understanding of them shaped the community of believers. By word of mouth they were passed on from one group to another and from generation to generation. Even after they became fixed in written records, it was the reading aloud and retelling of them that was felt to be of paramount importance. They could never be only words on a page. Just as they were forged in the circumstances of personal encounter and sharing, so they continued to demand human agents—voices of conviction which would give them breath as living words. Spoken again, the stories were alive in the context of contemporary lives.

What we are saying is that the stories and oracles, songs and prophecies do not find their true purpose and value outside the community. Always they need the community to give them their living setting and significance. This does not mean that individual members of the community cannot read the scriptures privately for their own benefit, but even then they do so as participants in the community. Their reading is informed by their community experience, and the influence of their reading is carried back into their common life with other Christians.

We recall our analogy with family anecdotes and sayings. Similarly do the biblical stories tell us who we are as inheritors of the early Jewish and Christian traditions. Together we use them as touchstones to help us interpret and understand our present experience. The awareness that we are called to a freedom which demands that we worship nothing other than what is of ultimate worth is tested by our re-hearing of the exodus experience. The Israelites left the security of slavery to begin their risky pilgrimage with nothing to hang onto but their hope in God. What are our slaveries and what is the character of our hope?

Or again, all our sufferings are now seen from the perspective of the cross. God, we believe, has shared this completely—not only in the color and pageantry—but also in the agony and heartbreak of our lives. From such stories emerge our life-interpreting symbols and metaphors: the broken bread and wine outpoured, the wilderness and the crossing of the Jordan River into the promised land.

Why just these stories and not others too? Why not add stories from other cultures and our own experience? We shall soon wish to comment on the special character of revelation which the Bible is felt to bring, but for the moment it is sufficient to recognize that early Christian peoples had to agree upon a core of stories if the narratives were to serve their community-forming and -sustaining purposes. As Christianity began to spread and as a variety of new documents were written—some claiming divine inspiration, it became evident that there had to be a limit or rule. This came to be called the *canon* of agreed-upon scriptural writings. The Gospels, letters, prophecies, psalms, wisdom books and histories within this canon were felt to have the breadth, authenticity and depth necessary to cover and to preserve the foundational experiences of Christianity and of the Judaism in which it is based.

The existence of a canon or finished Bible does not mean, however, that there should be no more stories and no further revelation. While no more stories may be added to the common stock shared by everyone, various branches of Christianity have their own narratives about great events and individuals: the beginnings of their church community, their martyrs and saints. Actually it is the very function of the biblical stories not only to help interpret these new experiences, but to help them come into being. Biblical parables of surprising forgiveness and joy, or of calamity interpreted as new opportunity, are meant to help shape fresh parables. Oppressed peoples see themselves coming out of slavery like that in Egypt to find their freedom. A Francis seeks to pattern his life after his Lord's. Ugandan martyrs go to their deaths with Jesus' words of forgiveness on their lips.

The biblical narratives are, then, what we might call the master stories of the Christian faith. As they are heard with new ears, they are meant to offer experiences which the total community can in some sense relive. They are intended as the model stories guiding the interpretation of lives lived in community and inspiring the formation of new stories of grace and courageous belief.

Revelation

Revelation is an experience in which God is perceived to be acting and communicating with us. There are a number of ways of understanding such experiences. Among them this parallel analogy may be helpful when we are reading or hearing the scriptures.

I am in an art gallery and something about a particular painting catches my eye. I come closer and find myself drawn into a relationship with the artist's vision. Observation deepens to insight as my own memory and imagination are brought into dialogue with the painter's perspective and interpretation. On occasion the experience can become still more absorbing. I forget where I am and, to a point, who I am. I am caught up, no longer conscious of myself as one standing with my head tilted and mouth ajar. A kind of alchemy

7

has happened—something new, something which seems to me greater than the sum of my own perception and the artist's skill. People often speak later of such experiences as seeming like gifts.

Probably we would not yet wish to call this revelation. But what if the experience takes a still stronger hold on me? Not only do I perceive something about myself and life's possibilities which I have never fully realized before, but this insight seems to penetrate the relative character of all other circumstances. Although I may well find words in which to frame this perception difficult to come by, I feel I am beholding what is fundamentally true and essential to life. More than this! The gift implies a giver. I am not only seeing anew, I am being seen. The painting—or whatever the experience—has become a window.

All analogies have their shortcomings. This one might tend to make us think of revelation as a rather esoteric experience. Bible stories, however—like many a good painting—are made up of life's basic materials. One can sniff the dust on the road and taste loneliness and fear. Jesus' parables, for example, seem deliberately to point to daily problems and opportunities. At meals, at everyday work, in situations of desperate need, hostility and love people may suddenly be encountered by what Jesus speaks of as the kingdom or reign of God; that is, God's ruling love and justice in the world.

The stories are not meant to draw us away from reality but to offer what we might call boundary or frontier experiences. The reign of God, Jesus insists, is breaking into the world of human events—becoming part of our stories. With eyes that truly see and ears that really hear we may participate in the stories in such a way that at the heights and depths of experience we can be encountered by God.

In this sense the hearing of the Bible may be compared to the disciples' experience of Jesus. In and through the most human of circumstances God begins to be disclosed. The stories invite us to participate—to be the unhappy prodigal son who thinks his father will only take him back if he makes a legal arrangement with him; to be the father when he sees his long-absent son coming home; to be the elder son whose sense of worth and place is threatened by the love shown his brother. As sharers in the story something happens to us: what the Bible describes as repentance, which means a changing of heart and mind—a regret for past wrongs, but, more importantly, a turning of one's whole being and a new hope for life. We experience both challenge and opportunity, judgment and grace.

8

Not by any means will all this hearing and insight take place in church. Yet Christians do need a place and a time where the master stories can be shared, and they can respond to them with their own words, stories, songs and actions. Sometimes the revelation may only occur later when a similar experience is lived through. There are other occasions, however, when the hearing can there and then take on a sense of participation, both with the members of one's immediate community and with those through whose lives the stories first took shape. Together with them one becomes aware of the possibility of God active through the words—especially within the stories which from the first and repeatedly thereafter have been experienced as revelation. These are then recognized as records and interpretations of encounters with God. They are no longer what someone else says is revelation. They are revelation for us. Through these events and words God is made known in human life.

Powerfully this can happen at Good Friday and Easter. But it may also be known in hearing Paul's words about the character of love or in the prophet's dream of a new Jerusalem. Or again, for many Christians, the most familiar re-creation of revelation takes place in the setting in which other Bible stories are often heard—the Lord's Supper or Holy Communion: "Do this in remembrance of me."

Foreignness and Ambiguity

Two problems often arise when discussing the reading and hearing of the Bible. While both of them present difficulties, they also can be recognized as opportunities.

Because the biblical narratives and other materials were given expression in cultures very different from our own, they can frequently seem foreign to our ears. They involve customs and ways of looking at the world which are not always easy for us to understand or share in.

We cannot simply pass over these obstacles. Thoughtful reading and hearing often requires background information and help with interpretation. This is one of the reasons that church leaders need to be educated and skilled in assisting others toward understanding.

There is, however, a significant asset in the foreign character of the Bible. We can make a comparison with science-fiction literature which usually takes us in the other direction—to a strange world of the future. Yet good science-fiction writings do not, at their heart, ask us to live in unreality. Like the biblical stories they can interest

9

us and stir our imaginations because they tell us things that are true about our hopes and values which reach across distances of time and varying cultures. We become part of the stories because we are hearing not just about other characters but also about ourselves. We perceive truths concerning our lives which belong to us in our present circumstances but which also transcend them.

Such stories and visions help us to gain perspective on our ways of viewing the world—reminding us that our viewpoint is itself relative and highly conditioned by many temporal factors, including the customs and conventions of our particular society. We have, we come to realize, a better chance of sharing with our contemporaries of different cultures and backgrounds because our common stories are somewhat foreign to us all. We are also given a greater vision with which to judge our failures to strive for ideals which surpass our limited sense of self. We are no longer quite so bound by the present and are more open to the future and its changes.

In these ways the stories of the Bible can be both simple and profound. Often they invite a child's attention, while yet they lure the seeking mind and heart to and beyond the limits of their knowing.

At the same time the Bible can present understandings in ways which may seem to us ambiguous—at first a little confusing and even contradictory. To take but one example, in some passages the reign of God is spoken of as though it has already begun. At other times its coming seems to be off in the future. Yet, as soon as we stop to think about it, we realize that this is the way it must be. God is present in human life, but not so that we fully comprehend God's activity. The fullness of God's presence and of our understanding about how God is now in the world awaits us in the future.

The Bible is a blend of many different kinds of truth and levels of meaning; actual events and their interpretation, legends, myths and poetry. This doesn't always make it easy to understand, but it does offer more excitement and mystery—truths at the boundaries of human comprehension. We are drawn through surface and literalistic understandings toward more fundamental meaning.

God cannot be held by any words. The words always point beyond the stories they tell. The Bible does this by means of metaphor and imagery, by gaps and surprises in the stories, by stressing judgment in one place and mercy in another. At times the stories seem meant deliberately to scandalize our limited notions about being good in order to impel us toward a sense of love and justice which outreaches our ideas about goodness. Our human thoughts about God and the significance of life are bound to be too small. The Bible will not let us alone with that.

Additional Reading:

Those who wish to pursue the subjects we have touched upon may readily do so by means of articles on particular or general subjects in one-volume Bible commentaries or biblical dictionaries. Several of these are listed at the conclusion of the next chapter. One may want to trace the story of the development of the biblical canon and note how the number of books and their order differs slightly in several of the Christian traditions. Of major importance is the question of the Apocrypha—a collection of books which for the most part were written a century or two before New Testament times. In the Episcopal Church these writings are understood to be part of the Bible but are not regarded as of equal status with the Old and New Testaments.

The three volumes of *The Cambridge History of the Bible* are of much value in understanding how the Bible came to be and the history of its use and interpretation. The volumes are published by the Cambridge University Press in London and New York: Volume I, *From Beginnings to Jerome*, edited by P. R. Ackroyd and C. F. Evans (1970); Volume II, *The West from the Fathers to the Reformation*, edited by G. W. H. Lampe (1969); Volume III, *The West from the Reformation to the Present Day*, edited by S. L. Greenslade (1963). In briefer, helpful scope is *The Bible for Today's Church* (in the Church's Teaching Series) by R. H. Bennett and O. C. Edwards, published in 1979 by the former Seabury Press, New York.

Issues of the history, authority, and inspiration of the Bible are dealt with in *Anglicanism and the Bible*, edited by F. H. Borsch (Morehouse-Barlow, Wilton, Conn.: 1984). See also Darrell Jodock's *The Church's Bible: Its Contemporary Authority* (Augsburg Fortress Publishers, Minneapolis: 1989).

The Gospel as History, edited by Vilmos Vajta (Fortress Press, Philadelphia: 1975) is helpful with respect to recognizing how the Bible has always been interpreted within the context of the Christian community's life and needs. See especially the articles by Jür-

11

gen Roloff and André Benoit. Useful also on this and related points is O. C. Edwards' *How Holy Writ was Written* (Abingdon Press, Nashville: 1989).

Those who wish to follow up on several of the thoughts about stories, parables, and the reign of God outlined in this chapter may read my *Many Things in Parables: Extravagant Stories of New Community* (Fortress Press, Philadelphia: 1988).

Joseph P. Russell's *Sharing Our Biblical Story* (Morehouse Publishing, Wilton, Conn.: revised edition 1988) is valuable for insights into the readings and particularly for their use in Christian education.

Suggestions to Those
Who Read in Public

Whenever we read the Bible to other persons we are in some measure interpreting it to them. No matter how neutral we may try to be, we cannot help coloring our reading with our understanding of the meaning and significance of the passage. One phrase receives more emphasis than another. Here we pause slightly—if only because it seems a natural place to draw a breath. Even our accent and posture will have some effect on others. If those listening know us personally, at least subconsciously they are bound to be aware that *that's old Fred reading. I saw him yesterday at the store.*

At first it may bother us to realize this. Who are we to be speaking the Word of God and interpreting it? Yet we then, of course, recognize that this is the way it must be and always has been. God speaks to us through human lives. Preeminently in Jesus, who expressed the divine Word in a decisive fashion in his life, and then through the humanity of others, God chooses to be in the world.

Aware of this, we want to do as well as we can. We do not wish to inject our personality so as to detract from the meaning of the words. On the other hand, since the readings can only be articulated through our persons, we want to prepare and speak in such a way that others will share with us in the meaning and significance of what is happening.

Reading with understanding. Perhaps the most important preparation we can do is to achieve for ourselves the best possible understanding of the passage. Obviously we will be helped considerably by a general knowledge of the Bible. As we have opportunity, we will want to read books concerning the background of the scriptures, and perhaps take courses about the Bible. Information with respect to the culture and the original languages will be useful to us. Looking through a set of maps and learning about climate and landscape can deepen our appreciation of particular lessons.

Some passages will be more difficult for us than others. A lesson from one of the prophets may make us want to do a little extra reading about the prophet. Any words we are unclear about should send us either to a regular dictionary or a special dictionary for biblical words.

The larger setting around the passage is usually quite important to its understanding. One should read what comes before and after. In many cases those who hear the lesson may be quite unaware of this context, but a reader's added sense of understanding can convey something of its significance to them.

One of the best forms of study a lector (which is another word for reader) can undertake is to read the lesson (or lection) in more than one translation. At first this may seem a little confusing. You will find that each version has had to do a little of its own interpretation. Different words are used in various translations giving different nuances of meaning. The punctuation may even vary slightly. It surprised me when I learned that the early manuscripts of the Hebrew scriptures and the New Testaments had very little punctuation in them. For that matter it was not until later centuries that the present verse and chapter numberings were devised.

Most lectors need not be unduly concerned about these issues. We are privileged to be able to stand on the shoulders of scholars who have thought these matters through with great care and have usually come to a consensus about them. Some of the variations in translation can, however, provoke us to new insights and reflection about the meaning.

Which version to use? The comparison of translations will help us to recognize that the version we read from does make a difference. Obviously we would not want to use a translation that pays little attention to basic historical questions involving the text. Fortunately there are a number of fine translations of the Bible into English available today so that our reasons for making a selection can depend on other concerns.

It may be that you will not have much choice in the matter. A particular version may be customary in your congregation and, at least for the present, a change is not under consideration. There is much to be said for a thoughtful and established decision in this area. It can be a great help to a congregation to become familiar with a particular translation. Surely it is not the best practice to have everyone reading from whatever Bible is convenient or happens to be a favorite, especially if this is based on the idea that it hardly matters.

Most of us will, however, want to have some familiarity with the major translations available today. We may in this way be helped to decide which version is most suitable for a particular congregation or form of service. Here a few comments are offered, but there is no substitute for doing one's own reading and comparing.

The King James Version (KJV), also known as the *Authorized Version* (AV). This translation, which itself has gained a kind of sacredness due to the power of Elizabethan-Jacobean English and its long usage, will continue to have a prominent place among English–speaking Christians. Some of its vocabulary and expressions, however, will not be directly comprehensible to most modern listeners.* In addition, since 1611 there have been quite a few advances in our knowledge concerning the actual words written by biblical authors. As an example, in 1 John 4.19 the KJV reads: "We love him (God) because he first loved us." We now know it is far more likely that this disciple originally wrote, "We love, because he first loved us." The difference in the absence of one word is subtle and profound.

The Revised Standard Version (RSV) of 1952 is now available in a new edition as *The New Revised Standard Version* (NRSV, first published in 1990). This is probably the most frequently used modern English Bible. While it retains much of the language and cadence of the King James Version, it makes use of better knowledge of the original texts and avoids outdated words. The NRSV seeks to use inclusive language in passages in which the original text was meant to be inclusive. The soundness, familiarity, and widespread use of the RSV and now the NRSV commend it for regular reading in many churches.

The New American Bible (NAB) of 1970 is now available in a revised version (NABrev), the revision of 1987 mainly focusing on the New Testament. Like the New Jerusalem Bible, this contemporary Roman Catholic translation follows the order of the Septuagint and

---

*This is most notably the case in a number of the prophetic books and in several of Paul's epistles where the translators' determination to give a word–by–word rendering of the original languages has further obscured the sense of the English for contemporary readers and listeners. On the other hand, the KJV translation of some of the narrative portions of the Bible has never been bettered.

Vulgate by intermingling the Apocrypha or deutero-canonical writings with those of the Old Testament. This can be somewhat confusing to those used to having the Apocryphal books grouped between the Old and New Testaments. The NAB is based on the best research and is attentive to modern use of the English language in the United States without losing a sense of the traditional dignity of the scriptures in English. At times, however, the language does seem unnecessarily formal, perhaps especially in its choice of words of Latin or Greek derivation instead of Anglo-Saxon provenance. Only in a very few cases have doctrinal issues affected the translation.

The Revised English Bible (REB) is a new version (1989) of the New English Bible (NEB) of 1970. The NEB was originally not intended for public reading, but its popularity has caused this thorough adaptation which is meant for public use. American readers will find some phrases or words more familiar to the British, and no careful effort has been made to deal with gender exclusive language, which is sometimes found even when not present in the original languages.

The New Jerusalem Bible (NJB) is also a new version (1985) of an older translation, the Jerusalem Bible (JB) of 1966. The JB was largely a translation from a French–language Bible. The NJB comes directly from the Hebrew, Aramaic, and Greek. With its extensive notes, the NJB is intended more as a study Bible than a Bible to be read publicly, but because the translators have a different touchstone than the English versions, many passages in the NJB have a remarkable freshness for English–language ears.

Today's English Version (TEV) or the Good News Bible of 1976 (The New Testament portion is also published in an edition entitled *Good News for Modern Man*). This translation is based on sound versions of the original texts and makes a determined effort to translate the scriptures into basic English with a sense of modern vernacular usage and relatively simple sentence structure. At times the translators' determination to "make sense" causes the TEV to cover up ambiguities that are present in the original writings, but its directness can unstop ears which have heard the same versions read over and again.

The New International Version (NIV) of 1978 is a translation by an international group of conservative Protestant scholars. It seeks fidelity to the original languages while rendering them in a clear and natural contemporary English style. Little attention is given to the avoidance of unnecessary masculine pronouns and other language.

This list is not meant to be exhaustive. Other translations have their values, but for the present the versions mentioned above are most likely to be used for public reading.

Know the Bible to be Used. Whatever version is to be used, the passage should be read over enough times so that one becomes familiar with it. When possible, read ahead of time in the actual book you are to use so that you can be familiar with the location of the passages on the page—where it begins and ends. (This is especially important if the passage is composite; that is, made up of verses which are not all consecutive.)* It is to be hoped that you will be reading from a Bible with large enough type so that you will not need to stare intently at the page with your head lowered in order to read. The Bible should also either be held up with the hand or elevated on a lectern so that the voice can be properly projected.

If possible mark ahead of time your place in the Bible with a card or piece of paper. I remember hearing the Dean of a large English cathedral muttering "Darn Habbakuk, darn Habbakuk," as he tried to locate this relatively minor prophet in the middle of a service.

Punctuation. One should carefully rehearse the proper punctuation of a sentence, especially noting where pauses are necessary to help establish the meaning. Questions and quotations need careful attention. Look, for instance, at this passage from the story of the healing of the paralyzed man (Mark 2.8–12 in the NRSV):

> At once Jesus perceived in his spirit that they were discussing these questions among themselves; and he said to them, "Why do you raise such questions in your hearts? Which is easier, to say to the paralytic, 'Your sins are forgiven,' or to say, 'Stand up, and take your mat and walk'? But so that you may know that the Son of man has authority on earth to forgive sins"—he said to the paralytic—"I say to you, stand up, take your mat and go to your home." And he stood up, and immediately took the mat and went out before all of them; so that they were all amazed and glorified God, saying, "We have never seen anything like this!"

---

*There are now in print several lectionary texts which set out the passages of the Bible to be used for the Sunday lessons and other major days, including the composite readings. A version using the RSV Common Bible is published by the Church Hymnal Corporation, 800 Second Avenue, New York, N.Y. 10017.

Read carefully, this passage can make good dramatic sense. Read without care, it will be confusing.

For another example of a passage requiring thoughtful attention to punctuation and sentence structure, look at Isaiah 40.6–11.

Complexity of argument. A passage such as Romans 3.1–9 illustrates both the importance of punctuation and other issues we have discussed to this point. Only a reader who had intelligently rehearsed this lesson could convey its difficult message to a congregation.

Irony and Satire. In Paul, Job, several of the prophets, and occasionally elsewhere (not infrequently in the words of Jesus himself) we find irony in the Bible—statements which are meant to be understood with implications other than what is actually said. The Epistle of James 2.16 provides a good example: the author asks whether someone with faith but lacking in good works can help a needy brother or sister by merely saying, "Go in peace, be warmed and filled," without giving any material assistance. Only an ironic tone of voice would convey the author's devastating criticism of such an attitude.

Satire (which often includes the use of sarcasm as well as irony) is found more frequently in the Old Testament than the New. A delicious illustration is the satire of idolatry in Isaiah 44.9–20.

Pronunciation. Most of us have suffered through a reading in which the lector obviously had little idea of how to pronounce the names of persons or places. If the lection should happen to include a genealogy or references by Paul to a number of his friends (or, in fair warning, have a look at the lesson for the third Sunday after Epiphany in Year C, Nehemiah 8.2–10), it may sound as though the unprepared reader had caught his or her tongue in a revolving door.

Even those who are most versed in the scriptures have to check from time to time on the normal pronunciation of unfamiliar biblical words. An authoritative source in which this can be done is *The Interpreter's Dictionary of the Bible* (see Additional Reading below). There are one-volume dictionaries which give similar assistance (e.g., *The New Westminster Dictionary of the Bible*) and a number of editions of the Bible offer special aids to pronunciation. If none of these resources is available, one should seek out a more experienced reader for advice.

Speaking clearly. It is necessary when reading in public to enunciate more distinctly than most people do in normal conversation. Without exaggeration each word and syllable should be given its full

18

expression. To be guarded against is the tendency to run words together and to slur their endings. Final *ings*, and *t's* and *d's*, especially when followed by an *s*, can too easily be omitted ("the hos' of the Lord went out" instead of "hos*ts*") and the meaning obscured. Many of us are also inclined to drop our voices at the end of sentences. This may be permissible in private conversation where it can be used for effect, but it is not effective in public speaking.

Pace. If we are conscious of the value of proper pauses and clear enunciation, we will probably speak at about the right speed—more slowly than normal conversational tempo, but without exaggeration. Some inexperienced readers, perhaps anxious to be done, have a tendency to rush which can best be overcome by a strong desire to be heard clearly and to share the meaning of the reading. A proper sense of the right rhythm for each sentence will help us gain a good feeling for pace.

Tone of voice and volume. Likely we have all heard lectors who adopt *stained glass* voices for reading in church. They sound affected and *put on* as though they were trying to make us believe in their piety. They may only be attempting to share a sense of the sanctity of the scriptures, but the Bible needs no special treatment. One's normal voice, with due care for the suggestions made in this chapter, is quite appropriate for the reading of the Bible.

With a congregation of any size one will, of course, need to raise the volume of one's voice. A good rule of thumb is to speak just a little louder than seems necessary to be heard by a person in the back pew. If, however, it feels as if you are bellowing or shouting, the strain on your voice will probably be uncomfortable both for you and those listening. None of us needs to shout to be heard. The best way to overcome this tendency is to recognize that effective use of the voice actually involves the whole body and especially our chest, lungs and diaphragm. One does not speak with only the mouth and throat. If you read slowly enough, stand erect and breathe regularly enough to keep a sufficient volume of air in the lungs, you should have sufficient natural power in your speech. It often helps to think of your voice as rising from the center of your chest (if you will, the center of your person) as you read to others.

The use of electronic sound equipment will overcome difficulties in large churches but can create special problems unless you are familiar with it. If at all possible, practice with the microphones, switches (if any), and speakers before using them in public.

The extremes of a flat monotone, on the one hand, and an exces-

19

sive amount of stress and raising and lowering of the voice, on the other hand, are to be avoided. The former loses the hearer's attention while the latter may result in a kind of sing-song which becomes boring in its own way. Again, a good understanding of the reading and attention to the natural rhythm of the sentences should give a sense of the proper intonation.

A proper balance should also be struck between the tendency to give a dramatic reading performance and the avoidance of any appropriate emotion in the voice. The overly dramatic rendering will call more attention to the reader than to the reading. Yet to read without any emotion would be neglectful of the meaning.

Practice. All these suggestions imply a need to practice and to benefit from thoughtful responses to our public reading. Even those who have read for years can learn to be more effective.

You might have friends listen to you and make their comments. If you can obtain the services of a voice teacher, the benefits could be considerable. Listening to yourself on a tape recorder can help with tone and enunciation.

You will want to practice in the building where you are to read. You need, however, to be aware that at least many of the echoes or reverberations which are heard in an empty building are happily absorbed by the presence of a number of human bodies. These same bodies, together with the little noises a crowd of people makes, will mean, however, that you have to speak a bit more loudly before a congregation than in an empty building.

Interruptions and Disturbances. No one who reads in public can do so for long without experiencing the crying child, the coughing fit in the front pew, a noisy airplane, or some other disturbance. When such incidents occur, it is often best to raise your voice slightly and to continue confidently. Hearers are as used to disturbances as you are, and they will probably have little difficulty in giving their major attention to the reading. Only if the disturbance should become too great for the reasonable attention of most of those present, will you want to wait until the noise has passed or the situation been dealt with.

Errors. All of us make mistakes from time to time in reading. Words of apology or exaggerated gestures of dismay only call all the more attention to them. If the error is relatively slight, it is best to carry on, trusting that the attentive hearer will supply the necessary meaning. Otherwise one should simply repeat the word or phrase correctly. In a few cases, when one has somehow started the sentence with an incorrect sense of its meaning, it may be necessary to go back and repeat the entire sentence.

Prayer. Before you prepare for your reading and before you read, you may wish to say a prayer asking for the guidance and wisdom of God's Spirit to help you focus on the words of scripture and on those with whom you will be sharing the opportunity to hear these words as a new insight and inspiration for their lives.

Beginning and Ending the Readings. One wants to let the hearers become settled before beginning the reading. To start while people are still moving about many mean the loss of their attention for the crucial first words and perhaps, then, for the entire passage. In a number of churches it is also the practice to allow at least a few moments of silence after the reading before the next part of the service begins. Personally I find that this custom helps the words to find their response within me and create some application to my own life.

If introductions such as are found in this book are to be read aloud, they should normally precede any of the formal words of introduction such as "A reading from the letter of Paul to the Romans."

One should take special care to be sure that the beginning words of the Bible passage are as intelligible as possible. Sometimes the opening phrase will contain a pronoun in which case it is permissible and often wise to replace the pronoun with the proper noun— to begin, for instance, with "Jesus said to his disciples. . . ." rather than "He said. . . ." Sometimes a reading opens with a quotation where it would be helpful to begin, for example, "*Jesus said*, 'Truly, truly, I say to you. . . .'" On a few occasions a passage will commence in the middle of a story in such a way as almost to demand the addition of a beginning phrase. I have supplied a few suggestions in this regard in the notes to the introductions.

The rest of these remarks are directed primarily to those who are using the Book of Common Prayer of the Episcopal Church, and they should be read in conjunction with the following chapter.

Rubrics are printed in italics in most Prayer Books today. (Traditionally these directions were printed in red: rubric coming from a Latin word for red.) For each form of Morning and Evening Prayer and the Eucharist the directions given on pages 36, 74, 141–2, 322, 325–6, 354, 406, 888, 934–5 in the Book of Common Prayer are sufficiently clear to require little further elaboration.

What is important is that readers note that there are choices of introductions and closings involved and that they think through the manner of beginning and ending ahead of time. They should also be aware of the customs of a local congregation. One should not expect, for instance, to receive the response "Thanks be to God" to a concluding "The Word of the Lord" if the congregation is unfamiliar with this practice. The congregation may, on the other hand, be accustomed to this way of sharing in the reading and miss the opportunity if it is not given.

Readers should note that the Rite One and Rite Two forms for introducing the lessons vary slightly, the former making use of the older English end*eth*. Readers who find the variations and options at all confusing may wish to write the words out on a piece of paper ahead of time.

If some members of the congregation are accustomed to follow the readings in their Bibles and the information is not already printed in the bulletin, then it is certainly helpful to give the chapter number followed by the beginning verse number of the lesson.

Finally there is the question of how to refer to the various books of the Bible by title. Should one say "A Reading from Isaiah," or "The Book of Isaiah" or "The Book of the Prophet Isaiah"? Should one begin by referring just to "Matthew" or "The Gospel according to Matthew" or "of Matthew" or "of St. Matthew"? Does one say "A reading from the Letter (or Epistle) of Paul to the Galatians" or "A reading from Paul's Letter to the Galatians" or "A reading from the Letter to the Galatians" or just "A reading from Galatians"?* And do not some people, following the King James Version, always say "the Epistle of Paul the Apostle"?

Practices vary. My best advice, especially in the context of the Prayer Book services, is to make a consistent use of the titles of the

---

*This matter is further complicated for some who are aware of scholarly opinion indicating that the letters addressed to Timothy and Titus, and perhaps Ephesians and Colossians as well, were not authored by Paul but by disciples writing in his name. This was, of course, an accepted practice of the time and nothing of what we would consider deception would have been intended. Writers who did this were saying "This is what Paul would tell you if he were alive today." Some people wish to acknowledge this by omitting a reference to Paul in the title of these letters. The omission is, however, certainly not necessary, as in retaining Paul's name one is only following the same literary convention.

individual books as they are given in the New Revised Standard Version or the New English Bible.

Additional Reading:

Annotated versions of the Bible provide readers with various notes, aids, maps and often short introductions and articles on basic subjects. The Revised English Bible and the New Revised Standard Version are two of the several translations which are available in excellent study or annotated editions.

A one-volume Bible commentary is a helpful tool to have in one's own library. The following provide good basic information with a number of general articles.

The New Jerome Biblical Commentary, edited by R. E. Brown, J. A. Fitzmyer and R. E. Murphy (Prentice-Hall, Inc., Englewood Cliffs, N.J.: 1990). This work of Roman Catholic scholars contains a useful "Suggested Basic Bibliography."

Harper's Bible Commentary, edited by James L. Mays, (Harper & Row, New York: 1988).

Collegeville Bible Commentary, edited by Robert J. Karris (Liturgical Press, Collegeville, Minn.: 1983).

The Interpreter's One-Volume Commentary on the Bible, edited by Charles M. Layman (Abingdon Press, Nashville and New York: 1971).

Peake's Commentary on the Bible, General Editor, Matthew Black (Nelson and Sons, London and New York: 1962).

Articles on a host of particular subjects are provided by the four volume *The Interpreter's Dictionary of the Bible*, Editor, G. A. Buttrick (Abingdon Press, Nashville and New York: 1962) with an excellent supplementary volume (General Editor, K. R. Krim) published in 1976. In one volume is *The New Westminster Dictionary of the Bible*, Editor, H. S. Gehman (Westminster Press, Philadelphia: 1970). Eerdman's *Handbook to the Bible,* edited by David and Patricia Alexander, (Grand Rapids, Mich.: 1973) offers considerable information in an attractive format.

A volume with several purposes parallel to this book is William Sydnor's *Sunday's Scriptures: An Interpretation* (Morehouse Barlow, Wilton, Conn.: 1976). Reginald H. Fuller's *Preaching the New Lectionary: The Word of God for the Church Today* (The Liturgical Press, Collegeville, Minn.: 1971–74) provides a commentary on the lessons for Sundays based on the Roman Catholic lectionary (see chapter four). Written for the benefit of those who preach, it will also be found valuable by those seeking better to understand the lessons before reading them. Two books rather similar in purpose to Fuller's and also based on the Roman lectionary are Robert Crotty and Gregory Manley, *Commentaries on the Readings of the Lectionary* (Pueblo Publishing Co., New York: 1975) and Gerald S. Sloyan, *Commentary on the New Lectionary* (Paulist Press, New York: 1975).

William Syndor's *Your Voice, God's Word* (Morehouse–Barlow, Wilton, Conn.: 1988) offers wise and helpful guidance for those reading the Bible publicly.

There are a host of guides and commentaries on the Sunday lectionaries. *Proclamation: Aids for Interpreting the Lessons of the Church Year* (published by Augsburg Fortress is now in its fourth series) and may prove to be useful for readers of this book. *Preaching the New Common Lectionary*, originally published by Abingdon Press and scheduled for reissue in revised form by Trinity Press International beginning Advent 1992, can also be quite helpful although the lections will sometimes vary from those used by the Episcopal and several other churches.

Using the Lectionary

A lectionary (from the Latin word *legere, lectum* = to read) is a cycle of readings to be read on particular days. The instructions for the use of the principal lectionary in the Episcopal Church are to be found on page 888 (with related information on page 158) of the Book of Common Prayer. There follow in individual three-year cycles the lessons and a selection from the psalter for all Sundays, major festivals and other significant occasions.

The basis for this lectionary is the *Ordo Lectionum Missae* in use (with revisions) in the Roman Catholic Church since 1969. The adaptation of the form and many of the lessons of the *Ordo* by other major church traditions in North America represented an important ecumenical accomplishment and opportunity. Several of the Protestant churches are now using a further revised common lectionary. Sunday after Sunday many of the same passages from the Bible are now being read and reflected upon in a great number of the churches of our land. Throughout the Episcopal Church, whether the Eucharist or Morning Prayer (or perhaps on a few occasions Evening Prayer) be the principal service, the lessons are still taken from the same lectionary.

A second major benefit of this lectionary derives from the provision of a much larger selection of readings than was to be found in the older one-year lectionaries. Especially have the Jewish scriptures been given a more frequent and prominent place at the Eucharist. The congregation, the preacher and teachers are presented with a far greater opportunity to make use of the richness and diversity of the Bible.

Each set of three readings for a particular day has a lesson from the Old Testament or the Apocrypha. Its major theme is often related to the season of the church year (especially is this true during Lent) and will otherwise usually point toward the Gospel for the day. (During Easter this first lesson comes from the Acts of the Apostles while an Old Testament lesson is provided as an alternative.) If only two lessons are to be used at the Eucharist, the Old Testament lection may serve as the first lesson or be omitted. At

25

Morning Prayer the Old Testament reading is regularly the first lesson whenever two or three lessons are included.

The selection from the Psalter is, with the Gospel reading, usually common to most of the churches following this lectionary pattern. Often one can identify a major theme of the psalm oriented toward the season. It may sound in a different key a note from the Old Testament and/or the Gospel lesson. In a number of instances the possibility of using shorter passages from a particular psalm is indicated in the Episcopal Lectionary. This option is intended for Eucharists where a shorter selection between the lessons (normally after the Old Testament lesson and before the second lesson or Epistle) is felt desirable.* In this book I have composed summary statements about the psalter selections which can be employed for either the shorter or longer versions.

The second of the lessons is drawn from a New Testament writing other than the Gospels, most often one of the letters of Paul or another disciple. Except for major feasts, when the lesson is specifically related to the festival, these lections usually follow their own course of sequential readings and so are not tied directly to the Old Testament lesson or the Gospel of the day. During Advent and Lent, however, they are related to themes of the season, and there is then often a relatively explicit association with one or both of the other lessons. The same Epistle reading is often used by other churches with similar lectionaries.

One has several options as to the use of this lesson. When only two readings are included in the service, this lesson can be omitted, or it can become the first lesson followed by the Gospel passage. Or at Morning Prayer it can be the second of two lections. It can also serve as the only lesson read at Morning Prayer.

The Gospel passage always is included at the Eucharist and may be read as the only or the last lesson at Morning Prayer. Through Year A of the new lectionary Matthew's Gospel is read, Mark in B (with a few additional lessons from John), and Luke in C. On many important festivals and during much of Lent, Holy Week and the

---

*Those who desire to sing the gradual psalms responsively, perhaps together with alleluia verses before the Gospels, may wish to have the texts and instructions prepared for these purposes in *A Guide to the Lectionary* by Ann Brooke Bushong (Seabury Press, New York: 1978). The book also usefully sets out, in tabular form, excerpts from the Scriptures appointed for the day. Refrains for the psalms can also be found on the Scripture inserts for Sunday bulletins now used by a number of congregations.

Easter season the Fourth Gospel provides the Gospel passages for all years of the lectionary.

On a number of occasions the opportunity for longer readings is indicated by additional verse numbers within parentheses. These extended passages are intended for Morning Prayer but may be used at the Eucharist. One will probably find that the longer lections are best suited to services with two lessons rather than three.

The rubrics instruct that the three-year cycle always begins with year A on the first Sunday of Advent in years evenly divisible by three. Those with pocket calculators and/or church calendars will have no difficulty figuring out what is to happen next.* For convenience, however, I offer the following little table.

Advent until Advent	Lectionary	Ash Wednesday	Easter	Second Sunday after Pentecost uses Proper		
1990–1991	B	Feb 13	Mar 31	June 2	=	4
1991–1992	C	Mar 4	Apr 19†	June 21	=	7
1992–1993	A	Feb 24	Apr 11	June 13	=	6
1993–1994	B	Feb 16	Apr 3	June 5	=	5
1994–1995	C	Mar 1	Apr 16	June 18	=	6
1995–1996	A	Feb 21	Apr 7†	June 9	=	5
1996–1997	B	Feb 12	Mar 30	June 1	=	4
1997–1998	C	Feb 25	Apr 12	June 14	=	6
1998–1999	A	Feb 17	Apr 4	June 6	=	5
1999–2000	B	Mar 8	Apr 23†	June 25	=	7
2000–2001	C	Feb 28	Apr 15	June 17	=	6
2001–2002	A	Feb 13	Mar 31	June 2	=	4
2002–2003	B	Mar 5	Apr 20	June 22	=	7
2003–2004	C	Feb 25	Apr 11†	June 13	=	6
2004–2005	A	Feb 9	Mar 27	May 29	=	4
2005–2006	B	Mar 1	Apr 16	June 18	=	6
2006–2007	C	Feb 21	Apr 8	June 10	=	5
2007–2008	A	Feb 6	Mar 23†	May 25	=	3
2008–2009	B	Feb 25	Apr 12	June 14	=	6
2009–2010	C	Feb 17	Apr 4	June 6	=	5
2010–2011	A	Mar 9	Apr 24	June 26	=	8
2011–2012	B	Feb 22	Apr 8†	June 10	=	5
2012–2013	C	Feb 13	Mar 31	June 2	=	4
2013–2014	A	Mar 5	Apr 20	June 22	=	7

†Leap years

*These and other dates may also be calculated by using the Table on pages 884–85 of the Book of Common Prayer.

The Book of Common Prayer stipulates that Easter, the Ascension, Pentecost, Trinity Sunday, All Saints' Day, Christmas and the Epiphany are principal feasts and that their propers must always take precedence over any other day or observance. Introductions for the lessons for these days are provided at the appropriate time in the church year, except for All Saints' Day which is included at the end.

Three other festivals always take precedence when they occur on a Sunday. Introductions for the lessons of the Holy Name are provided between the First and Second Sunday after Christmas, while those for the Presentation and the Transfiguration follow at the end.

Because sizable congregations are to be expected on Ash Wednesday, Maundy Thursday and Good Friday introductions are also provided at the appropriate place in the year for the readings for these days.

FIRST SUNDAY OF ADVENT

First Lesson   Isaiah 2.1–5

In our Old Testament lesson **the prophet Isaiah sets forth a majestic vision of a time when people throughout the world will worship the Lord and live in peace with one another.** The mountain of the city of Jerusalem will be raised up to become a symbol of hope and justice to every nation. Many peoples will look to Jerusalem and to its holy mount Zion as the place from which God will issue God's word and law, bringing about an end to strife and warfare.

Psalm 122: A pilgrim's song of praise and prayer for the peace of Jerusalem

Second Lesson (The Epistle)   Romans 13.8–14

In this reading **Paul summarizes the heart of the law and urges a way of life in full awareness of the nearness of salvation.** All the commandments and all human responsibility for others are fulfilled by "loving your neighbor as yourself." Disciples must recognize that the nighttime of sinfulness is passing. The daylight, the time for new conduct and the following of Jesus, now comes.

The Gospel   Matthew 24.37–44

In our Gospel lesson **Jesus tells his disciples of the need for readiness because the Son of Man will come at a day and hour which no one knows.** People will continue to go about their usual affairs, when suddenly this time of judgment will happen. Disciples are to be ever watchful, imagining themselves like a householder whose alertness could prevent a robbery.

FIRST SUNDAY OF ADVENT

First Lesson   Isaiah 64.1–9a

The Old Testament lesson presents **a contrite plea to God for merciful justice.** The prophet recalls earlier times when the Lord's presence made the very mountains quake. Now the people have sinned grievously and are suffering for their wrongs. They can only pray that the Lord will remember them as God's children, God's creatures, and temper divine anger.

Psalm 80 (or 80.1–7): A lament and a plea to the Lord, the shepherd of Israel, that God will turn away divine anger and restore the people.

Second Lesson (The Epistle)   I Corinthians 1.1–9

In this reading **Paul greets the new disciples in Corinth, telling them of his gratitude to God on their behalf, and offering comfort and assurance.** Because they are sanctified in Christ these converts, together with those everywhere who call upon Jesus, have a vocation as saints. They are rich in spiritual gifts. Trusting in a faithful God, they wait for the great revelation of the Lord Jesus Christ.

The Gospel   Mark 13.33–37

In our Gospel passage **Jesus repeatedly urges his disciples to watch, to be ever ready for the time which will suddenly come.** To stress this urgency he uses a little story about servants, left in charge while their master is away. They do not know when he may suddenly return. Just so must disciples be on the alert for their Lord.

An introduction to a longer version of the Gospel, Mark 13.24–37, is given on p. 204.

FIRST SUNDAY OF ADVENT

First Lesson   Zechariah 14.4–9

In the Old Testament lesson **the prophet offers a dramatic vision of the coming of the Lord to Jerusalem and the beginning of the new age.** Like a great warrior the Lord shall appear on the Mount of Olives, the mountain a few miles east of the city over which the sun rises on Jerusalem. Then there will be continuous day, and Jerusalem shall be as a paradise from which living waters will continually flow. The Lord will reign and all will know the Lord.

Psalm 50 (or 50.1–6): The psalm tells of the majestic and righteous God who requires true sacrifice and thanksgiving of God's people.

Second Lesson (The Epistle)   I Thessalonians 3.9–13

In this New Testament reading **the apostle Paul expresses gratitude to God for his disciples in Thessalonica and tells these followers of his prayers for them.** He has heard a good report of their faith and love and their concern for him. He prays that he will soon see them again, and asks that they may grow in love and be established in holiness in preparation for the coming of the Lord Jesus.

The Gospel   Luke 21.25–31

In our Gospel lesson **Jesus tells his disciples of the awe-inspiring crisis to come, which they may also recognize as the beginning of the time of their redemption.** The heaven and earth will bear fearsome witness before the appearance of the heavenly judge, the Son of Man. As the budding fig tree foretells the advance of summer, so can all this calamity be recognized as a preparation for the drawing near of the kingdom of God. While in one sense the passage makes use of the language of poetry to describe the indescribable, its central intention is clear: the ultimate purpose and meaning of life will finally be revealed.

SECOND SUNDAY OF ADVENT

First Lesson   Isaiah 11.1–10

   In the lesson from the Old Testament **the prophet foresees a time when God will bring forth a righteous judge and a new spirit of peace in the world.** The wise and faithful judge will come from the stump of Jesse, that is from the line of the great King David whose father was Jesse. The Spirit of the Lord will be his as he defends the humble and slays the wicked. The new age of peace will extend even to the animal kingdom.

Psalm 72 (or 72.1–8): The psalm asks that God endow the king with compassionate justice and righteousness, and that his reign may extend over all nations and throughout all generations.

Second Lesson (The Epistle)   Romans 15.4–13

   In this reading **Paul points to several passages from the Jewish scriptures to show how God's promise that the Gentile peoples should come to praise God was being fulfilled.** The new Roman converts, whom Paul hopes soon to visit, are urged to live in harmony and to recognize the manner in which Christ's ministry has brought these prophecies to fruition. He is the root of Jesse, that is, the promised son of David, on whom their hope is to be set.

The Gospel   Matthew 3.1–12

   Our Gospel lesson tells of **the ministry of John the Baptist, his message of repentance and his prophecy of the mighty one to come.** John himself is the messenger of preparation foretold by Isaiah. He baptizes with water those who confess their sins and wish to change their ways, but he chastises those who do not show the fruits of repentance. Soon comes the one who will baptize with the Holy Spirit and with refining fire.

SECOND SUNDAY OF ADVENT

First Lesson   Isaiah 40.1–11

The Old Testament reading is **a message of comfort and new hope to God's people.** The time of exile in Babylon is coming to an end. A new way is made through the desert, and the mighty Lord comes bringing peace and pardon to Jerusalem. Though all human powers fail, the Lord's word will stand. Like a shepherd God will care for the people.

Psalm 85 (or 85.7–13): The psalm both celebrates and prays for the Lord's gracious favor, God's forgiveness, deliverance and justice.

Second Lesson (The Epistle)   II Peter 3.8–15a, 18

This lesson is a reminder that **the divine perspective on time can be very different from that of human beings.** Many wonder why the Lord seems so slow to fulfill the promises of salvation and judgment. God, however, is patient and has divine purposes. Still the day of the Lord will come suddenly bringing a new heaven and earth. Christians must live both in patience and with a zeal for righteousness and peace in readiness for that judgment.

The Gospel   Mark 1.1–8

The Gospel of Mark begins with the ministry of John the Baptist. He is the messenger spoken of in the scriptures, the voice which cries aloud in the wilderness. He is sent to prepare the way of the Lord through his call for repentance and baptism in water for the forgiveness of sins. The people flock to him, but he tells of a mightier one still to come who will baptize with the Holy Spirit.

33

SECOND SUNDAY OF ADVENT

First Lesson   Baruch 5.1–9

The Old Testament reading offers **a tender message of encouragement to Jerusalem, a vision of the gracious Lord bringing the people home from exile and leading them in glory.** Although this prophecy is said to be written by Baruch, a friend of the prophet Jeremiah, it actually comes from a period nearer to New Testament times and is included in writings known as the Apocrypha. Its imagery of hope and joy is, however, timeless and points to God's ultimate work of salvation.

Psalm 126: A psalm of joy and hope sung to the Lord who restores the fortunes of the people.

Second Lesson (The Epistle)   Philippians 1.1–11

In this lesson **Paul greets the new disciples in the town of Philippi, gives thanks for their sharing in the gospel, and prays that they may be found without fault on the judgment day of Christ.** It is likely that this message of affection and appreciative joy was written toward the latter part of Paul's ministry, perhaps while he was in prison. He expresses great confidence that the work of grace begun by God in his converts will be brought to fruition.

The Gospel   Luke 3.1–6

The Gospel of Luke sets the prophetic ministry of John the Baptist in the context of its time in history. It was customary during this era to date events with reference to the lives of rulers and well-known public figures. Within this history the word of God comes to John as he preaches his baptism of repentance. His ministry is in fulfillment of the words of Isaiah concerning the one who prepares the way of the Lord.

THIRD SUNDAY OF ADVENT

First Lesson   Isaiah 35.1–10

In the reading from the Old Testament **the prophet envisions a time of abundance and healing for Israel.** As when the people were led out of Egypt into the promised land, so will be this new return in the power of God. Retribution will fall upon the Lord's enemies, but there will be water in the wilderness for the redeemed. In words which are later used by Jesus to describe what is taking place in his ministry, the prophet foretells an age when the blind and deaf, the lame and dumb will be healed.

Psalm 146 (or 146.4–9): A hymn of praise to the Lord, who forms the world and rules in justice, who heals and cares for the needy.

Second Lesson (The Epistle)   James 5.7–10

This lesson is **an exhortation to patient expectation in preparation for the coming of the Lord.** One may learn from the farmer, who must wait for the crop to ripen, or from the prophets who bore suffering with patience. Such endurance excludes a grumbling blaming of one another. The Lord will come soon.

The Gospel   Matthew 11.2–11

In our Gospel passage **Jesus responds to a question from John the Baptist about his mission and then describes John's ministry.** Jesus' answer to John's question suggests that people must make up their own minds about his role while observing the healings that are taking place in accordance with ancient prophecies. Those who hear Jesus are also to recognize that John is a prophet and more: he is the one who prepares for the Lord's coming.

THIRD SUNDAY OF ADVENT

First Lesson   Isaiah 65.17–25

In the reading from the Old Testament we hear of **a blessed time when God will overcome many of life's shortcomings and frustrations.** A prophet probably wrote these words in a period after the people had returned from exile but while there was still much cause for discouragement. A new order will come for Jerusalem. No longer will children die young or workers not know the fruits of their labor. Even the animals will enjoy the new age.

Psalm 126: A psalm of joy and hope sung to the Lord who restores the fortunes of God's people.

Second Lesson (The Epistle)   I Thessalonians 5.16–28

As he concludes his letter to the church in Thessalonica, Paul exhorts the new converts to live joyfully and prayerfully in readiness for the Lord's coming. Although they are to test what they hear, the disciples are to be expectant to discover the Spirit in prophecy. Trusting in a faithful God, the followers of Jesus are to seek to avoid all forms of evil and to become holy in every way.

The Gospel   John 1.6–8, 19–28

In the opening passages of his Gospel **the fourth evangelist firmly characterizes the mission of John the Baptist: he is the forerunner and witness to the Christ.** He bears testimony to the one who is the light of all human life. John is not the Christ or a figure for Elijah or one of the other prophets. He prepares the Lord's way and baptizes, while even now the one whom John is unworthy to serve stands unknown in their midst.

For Psalm 126 Canticles 3 or 15 (versions of the Magnificat) from the Book of Common Prayer may be substituted. A longer version of the second lesson is I Thessalonians 5.12–28. For its introduction see p. 204.

THIRD SUNDAY OF ADVENT

First Lesson   Zephaniah 3.14–20

In the reading from the Old Testament **the prophet foretells a
time when the judgment of Israel will be ended and the mighty
Lord will bring victory and renewal to God's people.** The city of
Jerusalem and its holy mount Zion may rejoice and sing. All enemies will be defeated and the crippled healed. The fortunes of Israel
will be restored, and the nation will be praised by all peoples.

Psalm 85 (or 85.7–13): The psalm both celebrates and prays for the
   Lord's gracious favor, God's forgiveness, deliverance and justice.

Second Lesson (The Epistle)   Philippians 4.4–7

In this New Testament lesson **Paul invites the new disciples at
Philippi to exult in the Lord who is near at hand.** In prayer and
thanksgiving they need have no anxiety. God's peace, which is beyond human understanding, will keep their hearts and thoughts
in Jesus. Even though Paul was experiencing his own troubles and
may at this time have been in prison, this letter is often called "the
epistle of joy."

The Gospel   Luke 3.7–18

In our Gospel **John the Baptist preaches repentance to all those
who hear his call to baptism, and he tells them of the mighty one to
come.** It is not sufficient to claim to be children of Abraham. All who
are to escape judgment must learn to share with others and to be
just in their daily work. John himself is not the Christ but the servant of the one who will baptize with the Holy Spirit and a refining
fire.

For the psalm Canticle 9 from the Book of Common Prayer may be substituted. A
longer reading from Philippians (4.4–9) may be used. For its introduction see p. 204.

FOURTH SUNDAY OF ADVENT

First Lesson   Isaiah 7.10–17

In the Old Testament lesson **the prophet Isaiah insists that King Ahaz of Judah will receive a sign from God, whether he wants it or not, the sign of a young woman bearing a son to be called Emmanuel.** Ahaz was more inclined to depend on political alliances than on the Lord. Isaiah prophesied that, by the time the infant began to be able to make his own choices, the Lord would destroy Judah's immediate enemies, although afterward a new threat would come. Christians have seen the ultimate fulfillment of these prophetic words in the birth of Jesus.

Psalm 24 (or 24.1–7): As pilgrims go up to God's holy place for worship, they cleanse themselves and praise the just Lord who has created all things.

Second Lesson (The Epistle)   Romans 1.1–7

Paul greets the new disciples in Rome and summarizes the gospel message. The prophecies concerning one to be descended from King David in human terms, and declared Son of God through the power of the Holy Spirit by resurrection from the dead, have been fulfilled. The Lord Jesus Christ has given grace and the commission of apostleship to bring peoples of all nations to faith and obedience.

The Gospel   Matthew 1.18–25

The Gospel tells **the story of the birth of Jesus.** While she was betrothed to Joseph, Mary finds that she is bearing a child. But an angel tells Joseph not to fear: this is the work of the Holy Spirit. The baby is to be named Jesus, which means "The Lord saves." The evangelist perceives this birth to be the fulfillment of an ancient prophecy which told of a virgin who would bear a son. The narrative makes clear the divine origin of this child who will save the people from their sins.

FOURTH SUNDAY OF ADVENT

First Lesson   II Samuel 7.4, 8–16

In the opening lesson **the prophet Nathan receives the Lord's promise to David concerning the future of the kingdom.** David, at one time but a shepherd boy, has recently become king in Jerusalem. Now the Lord declares a close relationship with David and his heirs, as father to son. His will be an enduring kingdom. Christians perceive this prophecy to have reached its greatest fulfillment in Jesus, the king of the new Israel and Son of God.

Psalm 132 (or 132.8–15): A petition to the Lord to remember the promise to David of a son to reign after him and for a lasting kingdom.

Second Lesson (The Epistle)   Romans 16.25–27

In words which close his long letter to the community in Rome **Paul reminds the new Christians of the mystery now disclosed to all nations, bringing them to faith and obedience.** Although the secret had long been kept in silence, the promise of the eternal God has been revealed and is made known through the prophetic scriptures. Glory to God who enables disciples to stand firm in the good news of Jesus!

The Gospel   Luke 1.26–38

Our Gospel relates **the story of the visit to Mary by an angel: Gabriel tells her that she is to bear Jesus who will be called the Son of God.** This happens during the sixth month of the pregnancy of Elizabeth, a kinswoman of Mary, who will soon give birth to John the Baptist. Mary is assured of God's favor and that this is the work of the Holy Spirit in fulfillment of the prophecy to David of an eternal kingdom. The narrative points to the transcendent origin of this child born into history.

39

FOURTH SUNDAY OF ADVENT

First Lesson   Micah 5.2–4

The Old Testament lesson presents **an ancient prophecy which foresees the day when a new ruler shall come forth for Israel out of David's city of Bethlehem in Ephrathah.** The prophetic poem looks forward to the restoration of the Davidic dynasty after a time of hardship. In the Lord's strength this ruler will be like a shepherd to his people, and his dominion will be great. The early church heard the prophet's words as an oracle concerning Jesus.

Psalm 80 (or 80.1–7): A lament and a plea to the Lord, the shepherd of Israel, that God will turn away divine anger and restore God's people.

Second Lesson (The Epistle)   Hebrews 10.5–10

This New Testament reading describes **the purpose of Jesus' coming into the world—to make an offering in his body for our sanctification.** The opening words are taken from the fortieth psalm. Repeated ritual sacrifices are of no delight to God in comparison with the once and for all offering which Jesus made in obedience to God's will. So does Jesus cancel the rule of the law, on which ritual sacrifices were based, and establish a new kind of obedience.

The Gospel   Luke 1.39–49

The Gospel tells of **Mary's visit to her kinswoman Elizabeth, and this humble woman's song of thanksgiving to the savior God who has called her to be the mother of the Lord.** Elizabeth is herself pregnant with a child who will be John the Baptist. Even in her womb this baby is joyful in Mary's presence. All generations will call Mary blessed.

To the Gospel Luke 1.50–56 may be added. The introduction given is suitable for the longer reading, or one may add to the last sentence ". . . blessed by the just and merciful God."

40

CHRISTMAS DAY I

First Lesson   Isaiah 9.2–4, 6–7

Our Old Testament lesson is **a hymn of thanksgiving and hope of-fered at the birth of a new king in Jerusalem.** The prophet hails the one born to be the ruler of his people. His reign will end oppression and bring justice, righteousness and a lasting peace. Christians see these words coming to fulfillment in Jesus.

Psalm 96 (or 96.1–4, 11–12): A song of praise to the Lord in which the whole heavens and earth are invited to join.

Second Lesson (The Epistle)   Titus 2.11–14

This New Testament reading speaks of **the two comings of Christ: first in his sacrificial ministry for all people and then in glory.** He has enabled his disciples to free themselves from ways of evil. Disciplined and eager to do good, they look forward to the fulfillment of the hope God has given to the world in Jesus.

The Gospel   Luke 2.1–14

The Gospel presents **the story of the birth of Jesus.** He is born amid very humble human circumstances. A government registration program requires Joseph and Mary to go to Bethlehem, the city of David. Because there was no other place for them to stay, Mary lays her new son in a stable manger. An angel then appears to shepherds and announces the joyful news of the Savior's birth.

The Gospel can be lengthened by adding verses 15–20, in which case the last sentence above may be replaced with the following: "An angel announces the joyful news of the Savior's birth to shepherds who come to Bethlehem and report the angelic vision."

CHRISTMAS DAY II

First Lesson   Isaiah 62.6–7, 10–12

The Old Testament lesson is **an expression of great expectation and rejoicing: salvation comes to Jerusalem.** The prophet pictures watchmen on the walls of the city calling upon the Lord. Then the people stream forward to hear the Lord's proclamation. They will now be named the Holy People, Redeemed of the Lord, Sought Out, a City Not Forsaken.

Psalm 97 (or 97.1–4, 11–12): A hymn to the awesome Lord and Ruler who brings the fire of judgment and light for the righteous.

Second Lesson (The Epistle)   Titus 3.4–7

This New Testament reading is **a summary of the story of our salvation.** Not by our deeds, but through God's goodness and mercy, we experience the water of rebirth and renewal in the Holy Spirit. We are now heirs in hope of eternal life.

The Gospel   Luke 2.15–20

Our Gospel tells how **the shepherds, after the angelic vision which announced Jesus' birth, come to Bethlehem to see for themselves the promised child.** They share with Mary and Joseph the words of the angels. In this little baby, laid in a manger, they perceive the fulfillment of the song of the heavenly hosts. Glorifying and praising God, they return to their fields.

The Gospel may be lengthened by first using Luke 2.1–14. For an introduction to this longer reading see the Gospel for Christmas Day I with its added note.

CHRISTMAS DAY III

First Lesson   Isaiah 52.7–10

The Old Testament lesson heralds **a time of great joy as the Lord saves the people and brings deliverance to Jerusalem.** The long exile is at an end. The messenger proclaims the good news, "The Lord reigns." The watchmen of the city respond with shouts of triumph to see God's salvation.

Psalm 98 (or 98.1–6): A song of thanksgiving and praise to the victorious Lord who has made righteousness known and shown faithfulness to God's people.

Second Lesson (The Epistle)   Hebrews 1.1–12

In this reading **the Letter to the Hebrews begins with a declaration of Jesus' sonship. He is far above all angels at the right hand of God.** Previously God had spoken through the prophets, but now God expresses himself in the Son, through whom the world was created and who bears the stamp of divine being. After making purification for sins, he has taken his seat of greatest honor. A series of quotations from the Old Testament is used to show the Son's superiority to the angels who are the highest order of created beings.

The Gospel   John 1.1–14

This Gospel opens with **a hymn to the expression of God's very being, God's Word, who has now become flesh and lived among us.** Through the Word all things have their life. The word is the light of all humankind, and was witnessed to by John the Baptist. Although the world made by the Word did not recognize the Word, those who believe in the Word have been given the right to become children of God.

FIRST SUNDAY AFTER CHRISTMAS

First Lesson   Isaiah 61.10–62.3

In our Old Testament reading **the prophet joyfully responds on behalf of all God's people to the Lord's promises for a redeemed Jerusalem.** He is a messenger to those who are poor and have suffered many troubles. Now he feels himself clothed in salvation and integrity, like a bridegroom or bride. In the sight of all peoples this nation shall become like a fresh garden. The prophet will not keep silence until the deliverance of Jerusalem is known throughout the world.

Psalm 147 (or Psalm 147.13–21): A hymn of praise to the Lord who rules over nature and has shown faithfulness to Jerusalem and God's people Israel.

Second Lesson (The Epistle)   Galatians 3.23–25, 4.4–7

In this reading **Paul explains what the role of the law has been and how, in our new relationship of faith, we have become heirs of the Father.** Before the coming of Christ and justification by faith we were like small children who had to be closely watched. God's own Son was born a subject of the law. Through him we now are given the status of young adults coming into their maturity. We are enabled, through the Spirit of his Son, to call upon God with the same Aramaic word for Father that Jesus is remembered to have used, *Abba.*

The Gospel   John 1.1–18

The Gospel opens with **a hymn to God's Word, the expression of God's very being and the creative power of all life, who has now become flesh and lived among us.** The Word is the light of all humankind, and was witnessed to by John the Baptist. Although the world made by the Word, did not recognize the Word, those who did believe in the Word have been given the right to become children of God. The law came through Moses, but grace and truth come through the only Son who makes the Father known.

HOLY NAME
January 1

First Lesson   Exodus 34.1–8

Our Old Testament lesson describes how **the Lord proclaims God's sacred name and again gives to Moses the ten commandments, written on tablets of stone, to replace those which had been broken.** Furious at the people's idolatry, Moses had smashed the first tablets. In response to prayers requesting forgiveness and for a vision of God, the Lord is now awesomely present to Moses on the holy Mount Sinai. The words which tell of the Lord's compassionate, long-suffering and just character are repeated a number of times in the Old Testament.

Psalm 8: The psalmist glorifies the name of the Lord, sovereign of the earth and the magnificent heavens, who has made human life to have mastery over all other earthly creatures.

Second Lesson (The Epistle)   Romans 1.1–7

Paul greets the new Christians in Rome and tells of the apostolic mission given to honor Jesus' name. The prophecies concerning one to be descended from King David in human terms and declared Son of God through the power of the Holy Spirit by resurrection have been fulfilled. This message of faith is to be taken to all peoples.

The Gospel   Luke 2.15–21

Our Gospel tells how **the shepherds, after the angelic vision which announced the Savior's birth, come to Bethlehem to see for themselves the child who is to be named Jesus.** They share with Mary and Joseph the words of the angels. In this little infant, laid in a manger, the shepherds perceive the fulfilment of the song of the heavenly hosts. After eight days, in accordance with the law, the baby is then circumcised and given the promised name.

An alternative Second Lesson in Year A is Philippians 2.9–13. For its introduction see p. 205.

SECOND SUNDAY AFTER CHRISTMAS

First Lesson   Jeremiah 31.7–14

This Old Testament reading was originally composed as **a vision of hope, full of joy, for the restoration of the northern tribes of Israel.** The Lord will bring them all back from exile, including the weak and the infirm. As a father and a shepherd, he will comfort them and give them cause for great gladness.

Psalm 84 (or 84.1–8): A song of the pilgrims' happiness as they come to worship in the house of the Lord.

Second Lesson (The Epistle)   Ephesians 1.3–6, 15–19a

This New Testament lesson opens with **praise to God for God's blessings, together with thanksgiving and prayers that these spiritual graces may be continued.** In the beloved Son Christians have, since the beginning of the world, been given a destiny of holiness as God's sons and daughters. Paul prays for a spirit of wisdom and revelation so that the disciples' hearts may be enlightened to perceive the glorious hope of the saints.

The Gospel   Matthew 2.13–15, 19–23

Our Gospel is **the story of Joseph and Mary escaping to Egypt with the infant Jesus. They flee the jealous wrath of King Herod and are able to return to live in Nazareth only after his death.** These movements early in Jesus' life are seen as the fulfilment of prophecy. As God's Son, Jesus is brought out of Egypt just as were the people of Israel. The prophecy concerning Nazareth could have several sources, but the evangelist understands all things to be taking place according to God's plan.

The Gospel reading would best begin with a phrase such as, "After the wise men had departed, . . ." Two other Gospel passages may be used on this day. For an introduction to Luke 2.41–52 see p. 205; for Matthew 2.1–12 see p. 47.

THE EPIPHANY
January 6

First Lesson   Isaiah 60.1–6,9

In our Old Testament lesson **the prophet envisions the end of exile and the glorious restoration of Jerusalem.** Although darkness covers the earth, the Lord will be a light making God's people shine. To this radiance shall come the nations. Rich treasures will be brought from afar to honor the Lord.

Psalm 72 (or 72.1–2, 10–17): The psalm asks that God endow the king with compassionate justice and righteousness and that his reign may extend over all nations and throughout all generations. To him shall kings from distant lands bring gifts.

Second Lesson (The Epistle)   Ephesians 3.1–12

Here is set forth the great theme of Paul's apostolic commission: the revealed mystery that Christ's salvation extends beyond Judaism to include all peoples. The apostle is near the end of his ministry and in prison at the time of the writing of this letter. Now it is recognized as God's eternal purpose that the Gentiles are to be members of the same body. The wisdom of God is made known through the church even in transcendental realms.

The Gospel   Matthew 2.1–12

Our Gospel is **the story of the wise men from the east, who, guided by a star, come to worship the child born to be king.** Despite the wicked plotting of Herod, the Magi are able to bring their gifts to Jesus without betraying his exact location. Early Christians found in the rich symbolism and motifs of the story the fulfilment of both Old Testament prophecy and the dreams of many peoples. The meaning of this birth, amid terrifyingly human circumstances, enlightens and transcends human history.

FIRST SUNDAY AFTER EPIPHANY

First Lesson   Isaiah 42.1–9

In our reading from the Old Testament we hear of **the mission of the Lord's servant, the one whom God has chosen to bring forth justice and salvation.** This is the first of the "servant songs" which form a portion of the Book of Isaiah written at the time when the exile in Babylon was ending and the city of Jerusalem had begun to be restored. The servant is sometimes thought to be an historical individual, or is understood as an idealization of Israel. Christians see in the servant a prefigurement of the ministry of Jesus, who will become a light to the nations of the world.

Psalm 89.1–29 (or 20–29): The Lord is praised for faithful love and mighty justice. As a Father, God promises to the anointed servant David an everlasting kingdom.

Second Lesson (The Epistle)   Acts 10.34–38

In this reading we learn how **Peter recognizes that the good news, which Jesus began to proclaim after his baptism, now extends to all peoples.** At first Peter was slow to believe that God wanted him to bring the word to a non-Jew. But God has shown this to be the divine will, and Peter gladly responds to Cornelius, a Roman centurion, together with his family and friends.

Year A

The Gospel   Matthew 3.13–17

Our Gospel is **the story of Jesus' baptism.** John wonders why Jesus should come to him to receive a baptism for the remission of sins, but Jesus tells him that it is right and fitting. After he is baptized, the Holy Spirit is manifest. A voice from heaven proclaims who Jesus is with words which echo ancient oracles concerning the king and the calling of the Lord's chosen servant.

FIRST SUNDAY AFTER EPIPHANY

Year B

The Gospel   Mark 1.7–11

Our Gospel is **the story of Jesus' baptism.** John tells of the mightier one to come whose baptism will be with the Holy Spirit. Jesus is then baptized and the Spirit is manifest. A voice from heaven speaks to Jesus in words which echo ancient oracles concerning the king and the calling of the Lord's chosen servant.

Year C

The Gospel   Luke 3.15–16, 21–22

Our Gospel is **the story of Jesus' baptism.** Some people expected that John the Baptist might be the Christ, but he points to a yet mightier one to come whose baptism will be decisive. The Holy Spirit is then manifest and shows this one to be Jesus. A voice from heaven speaks to him in words which echo ancient oracles concerning the king and the calling of the Lord's chosen servant.

If verses 20–29 of Psalm 89 are used separately, then only the second part of the descriptive statement is appropriate.

The Gospel passage from Mark is best begun with a phrase such as, "In his preaching John the Baptist said, . . ."

SECOND SUNDAY AFTER EPIPHANY

First Lesson   Isaiah 49.1–7

In our Old Testament lesson **the servant of the Lord reflects movingly on his mission—its sorrows and frustrations, and God's high calling and promise to be with him.** The servant is sometimes thought to be an historical individual, or is understood as an idealization of Israel. This song was probably composed as the exiles from Jerusalem were preparing to return to their devastated city. Despite appearances, the Lord will make this servant a light to the nations.

Psalm 40.1–10: A prayer for deliverance and a song of thanksgiving to God who has saved the Lord's servant from great troubles and made it possible to sing God's praise.

Second Lesson (The Epistle)   I Corinthians 1.1–9

In this reading **Paul greets the members of the new Christian community in Corinth and offers thanksgiving for their growth in Christ.** He is writing from Ephesus some months after his first stay with the Corinthians, and he will shortly be concerned with many of their problems and questions. Now he reminds these disciples of their high calling and expresses his gratitude for their spiritual enrichment.

The Gospel   John 1.29–41

In our Gospel passage **John the Baptist declares who Jesus is. The next day two of John's followers become disciples of Jesus.** One of these disciples is Andrew who then brings his brother Simon Peter. John has led them to understand that Jesus is God's chosen one, the servant on whom God's Spirit rests. He is the Lamb of God who will be a sacrifice for the sins of the world.

SECOND SUNDAY AFTER EPIPHANY

First Lesson   I Samuel 3.1–10

In our Old Testament lesson we hear how **Samuel learns that it is the Lord who is calling to him.** Three times the boy Samuel misunderstands and thinks that it is his mentor Eli summoning him during the night. Finally Eli realizes it must be the Lord, and tells Samuel to be ready for the prophetic word which will be spoken to him.

Psalm 63.1–8: This psalmist seeks the Lord in whose presence there is sufficiency and contentment.

Second Lesson (The Epistle)   I Corinthians 6.11b–20

In this lesson **Paul is required to criticize a misguided understanding of Christian freedom which has been adopted by some of the Corinthians.** "All things are permitted me," is what some are saying, and evidently then interpreting their freedom in Christ to mean that they are so 'spiritual' that they can join with a prostitute without it doing any harm. But our bodies, Paul contends, like all the rest of us, have now been dedicated to Christ. They are temples of the Holy Spirit through which we may glorify God.

The Gospel   John 1.43–51

Our Gospel is **the story of Philip and Nathaniel becoming disciples of Jesus.** Nathaniel first doubts that the one whom Moses foretold could come from the virtually unknown town of Nazareth. But Jesus astounds Nathaniel by telling him what normal sight could not have disclosed. He then promises Nathaniel that he will have his own still greater vision, a heavenly revelation of the Son of Man as an intermediary between heaven and earth.

A longer Old Testament lesson, I Samuel 3.1–20, may be used. For its introduction see p. 205.

SECOND SUNDAY AFTER EPIPHANY

First Lesson   Isaiah 62.1–5

In our Old Testament lesson **the prophet continues to look forward to the full restoration of Jerusalem, hoping that the city may one day be a source of joy, as a bride is to her bridegroom.** It is some years after the return from exile, and Jerusalem has still not regained her glory. But the prophet trusts in the Lord. The city will become God's crown. The land will no longer be known as Forsaken, but will be called Married.

Psalm 96 (or 96.1–10): A song to the Lord, the Creator and Ruler of all, in which all the whole world is invited to join.

Second Lesson (The Epistle)   I Corinthians 12.1–11

In this reading **Paul commends spiritual gifts, but instructs the Corinthians in their proper use in the service of Jesus' lordship.** Spiritual gifts always present dangers as well as benefits, and there can even be false spirits. The Spirit of God will never cause one to believe that the earthly, crucified Jesus could be despised, for this same Jesus has become Lord of the church. It is also important to recognize that there are many different gifts of the one Spirit. All are to be used for the common good.

The Gospel   John 2.1–11

Our Gospel is **the story of the changing of water into wine during a wedding feast at Cana in Galilee.** The evangelist enriches the narrative with deep symbolism. As the first of Jesus' signs, this miracle points forward to his hour of greatest glory, when all things will be transformed by his death and resurrection. The best wine will be saved until last and will be given in astonishing abundance.

THIRD SUNDAY AFTER EPIPHANY

First Lesson   Amos 3.1–8

Our Old Testament reading is **a stern denunciation of Israel for its failure to live up to its calling.** The prophet Amos is appalled by the social and moral corruption he sees. The Lord had led Israel out of Egypt and chosen this people for a life of service. They instead have decided for iniquity. These words of judgment upon them are as inevitable as the analogies Amos then uses. Disaster comes from the Lord, and, when the Lord speaks, the Lord's message must be proclaimed.

Psalm 139. 1–17 (or 1–11): With marvelous wisdom God alone perceives the heights and depths of life.

Second Lesson (The Epistle)   I Corinthians 1.10–17

In this lesson we hear that **Paul is disturbed by news of factions in the young Corinthian church.** Apparently the new converts were dividing into groups based on who it was who baptized them and whose teaching they were following. They must instead be unified in Jesus in whose name alone they are baptized. Paul is grateful on this account that he himself has baptized very few of them, and that he does not preach with such eloquent wisdom that people would rely on him rather than the cross of Christ.

The Gospel   Matthew 4.12–23

The Gospel is **a summary of the early ministry of Jesus: his preaching, the calling of disciples and his acts of healing.** After the arrest of John the Baptist, Jesus withdrew to Galilee, an area in which many Gentiles lived. The evangelist perceives in this a fulfillment of prophecy and a foreshadowing of the church's mission to bring the light of the gospel to darkened lives. Two sets of brothers are called to leave their nets and become fishers of people.

THIRD SUNDAY AFTER EPIPHANY

First Lesson   Jeremiah 3.21–4.2

From the Old Testament we hear **a poem of moving repentance and God's forgiveness.** The people are weeping because of their evil ways, their idolatries and disobedience. The Lord invites them as wayward children to return and to live in uprightness and justice.

Psalm 130: A plea for mercy offered in patient hope to the faithful Lord.

Second Lesson (The Epistle)   I Corinthians 7.17–23

In this reading **Paul urges the Corinthians not to be concerned with outward signs or status.** Disciples can keep the commandments and serve the Lord in whatever circumstances they find themselves. Paul is not against taking opportunities such as the slave may find to gain freedom. But radical obedience to God is independent of the standards of the world's social order or, for that matter, of worldly religion.

The Gospel   Mark 1.14–20

Our Gospel records **the beginning of Jesus' ministry: his proclamation of the coming kingdom and the calling of his first disciples.** After the arrest of John the Baptist, Jesus returns to Galilee preaching the nearness of God's ruling and the need for a change of heart. Two sets of brothers are bidden to leave their nets and become fishers of people.

THIRD SUNDAY AFTER EPIPHANY

First Lesson   Nehemiah 8.2–10

The Old Testament lesson recalls **a great day in the history of Israel: in the restored city of Jerusalem Ezra gathers the people together so that they may hear and understand the law of Moses.** It would seem that many of the people were unfamiliar with their traditions, and this reading may have taken place at a time when their laws and stories had been newly gathered together and edited. We note the people's reverence for their scriptures, and the manner in which they are not only read but expounded to them, probably in their own language of Aramaic since the law was written in Hebrew.

Psalm 113: Praise to the Lord enthroned on high who lifts up the weak and lowly.

Second Lesson (The Epistle)   I Corinthians 12.12–27

In this passage **Paul describes Christians as the body of Christ. Each individual is a necessary part of the body.** Against any tendencies toward disunity, it must be remembered that all have been baptized into one body and have drunk of one Spirit. Just as there are different organs and limbs of the human body, so individuals have different abilities and ministries. But none can be dispensed with. They are all joined together to care for one another.

The Gospel   Luke 4.14–21

In our Gospel story **Jesus returns to Galilee and enters the synagogue in Nazareth. Here he gives what has been called his inaugural sermon.** He reads from the book of the prophet Isaiah. These words offer hope and good news to the poor, and tell of healing and freedom for the oppressed. This time, Jesus says, has begun.

FOURTH SUNDAY AFTER EPIPHANY

First Lesson   Micah 6. 1–8

In our Old Testament lesson **God contends with the people of God, reminding them of the saving acts done for them and instructing them in the good that God expects.** The very mountains and hills are called as witnesses. God led the people out of Egypt and through the wilderness in safety. Yet they sin. It is not animal or human sacrifices the Lord wishes, but that the people act in justice, with loving kindness and humility.

Psalm 37:1–18 (or 1–6): A psalm of advice to the wise, teaching them to avoid evil and wait patiently on the Lord in righteousness.

Second Lesson (The Epistle)   I Corinthians 1.26–31

In this reading **Paul directs the attention of the Corinthians to God's way of using what is weak and lowly—even what the world regards as foolish—to accomplish the divine purposes.** Paul emphasizes this understanding because a number of these new Christians had come to think of themselves as especially gifted, powerful and wise. As the cross has shown, however, God's ideas about what is wise and noble are often quite different from ours. Our only boast can be in the Lord.

The Gospel   Matthew 5. 1–12

The Gospel lesson is **the opening sayings of the Sermon on the Mount, words of both comfort and challenge.** The values of God's reign are quite different from worldly standards. Those who are to find blessing will know want and thirst, if not because of their own circumstances, then for the sake of others. Those who hunger for righteousness will find fulfillment, but first they must experience persecution.

For the introduction to a longer second lesson, I Corinthians 1:18–31, see p. 206.

FOURTH SUNDAY AFTER EPIPHANY

First Lesson   Deuteronomy 18.15–20

In our Old Testament reading **Moses promises the people that,
after his death, God will raise up another prophet for them.** The
people cannot face God directly but need an intermediary to speak
God's words. To him they must listen, while the false prophet, who
presumes to speak in the Lord's name, will die. In later centuries
this oracle was interpreted to mean that God would raise up one
final prophet to succeed Moses. Some early Christians believed
Jesus to be this new Moses.

Psalm 111: A song of praise to the mighty and awesome Lord who is
steadfast and full of compassion.

Second Lesson (The Epistle)   I Corinthians 8.1b–13

In this New Testament lesson **Paul gives counsel to the Corinthians who are unsure whether it is permissible to eat the meat of animals which have been sacrificed in pagan temples.** Since there is
only one true God, such sacrifices are really meaningless, and the
meat can be eaten in good conscience. Yet this understanding of
the issue must not be treated as superior *knowledge* with respect
to those whose consciences are still troubled. Out of love it is better
for those who believe themselves enlightened to avoid eating such
meat than to encourage weaker members to do what they regard as
sinful and so perhaps to be led back into paganism.

The Gospel   Mark 1.21–28

In our Gospel **Jesus both teaches and acts with authority.** His
teaching was more than interpretation of the law. It was a proclamation of the new possibilities of God's reign. He backed his words
with his actions. Unclean spirits recognized him and submitted to
his power to deliver a man from his disorder.

The lesson from Deuteronomy would best begin with the addition of a phrase such
as, "Moses said to the people, . . ."

FOURTH SUNDAY AFTER EPIPHANY

First Lesson   Jeremiah 1.4–10

From the Old Testament we hear **the story of the calling of Jeremiah to be a prophet of the Lord.** Jeremiah protests that he is inadequate to the task, but the Lord promises to be with him. He has been chosen to prophesy destruction and exile for Judah. Yet he will also help his people find a faith which can survive without city and sanctuary until they are one day brought back to Jerusalem.

Psalm 71.1–17 (or 1–6, 15–17): A prayer that God will continue to be one's refuge and stronghold.

Second Lesson (The Epistle)   I Corinthians 14.12b–20

In this reading **Paul gives instructions to the Corinthians on the best use of the gift of speaking in tongues.** Evidently there had been some extremism in the manifestation of this activity. Paul is grateful that he too has the gift of tongues, but it is useful in public worship only when it can be plainly interpreted. A few words clearly understood are of much more value for the building up of the church than many words spoken in tongues.

The Gospel   Luke 4.21–32

In our Gospel we hear how **Jesus encounters opposition in the synagogue of his own town of Nazareth.** The congregation admires his words, but is also perplexed because they know his human origins. Jesus recognizes that people are unlikely to expect a prophet from among their own, and he reminds them how Elijah and Elisha did certain of their miracles for non-Jews. These illustrations (which point to the later ministry of Christianity to the Gentiles) deeply disturb the congregation, and Jesus is forced to leave for Capernaum to continue his ministry.

The Gospel reading would best begin with a phrase such as, "Jesus began to say to those in the synagogue, . . ."

Year A

FIFTH SUNDAY AFTER EPIPHANY

First Lesson   Habakkuk 3.2–6, 17–19

In our Old Testament lesson **the prophet Habakkuk offers praise to the glorious Lord of the heavens for God's saving deeds on behalf of the people.** God moves forward like a mighty tempest; to God belong all the powers of nature. To the Lord who inspires such awe, the prophet prays for mercy. Even if all the crops should fail, the Lord will still be his strength and joy.

Psalm 27 (or 27.1–7): The psalmist expresses great trust and confidence in the Lord and asks always to be in God's presence.

Second Lesson (The Epistle)   I Corinthians 2.1–11

In this reading **Paul teaches the Corinthians that the wisdom of God is very different from the wisdom in which humans pride themselves.** Some of the Corinthians were apparently boasting of their Christianity as though it were powerful in terms of worldly wisdom. They even made fun of Paul for his lack of eloquence. The true power of God is, however, hidden from the ruling forces of the world, for it is discovered in a crucified Lord. This is revealed through God's own Spirit.

The Gospel   Matthew 5.13–20

In the Gospel lesson we learn that **disciples are like salt and as light to the world. They are to live even more righteously than the pious scribes and Pharisees.** Like a city set on a hill or a lamp on a stand Jesus' followers must show forth their good works to the glory of God. Jesus has not come to abolish the law and the prophets but to fulfill their purpose. Only those who go beyond the keeping of the law and are wholly committed to God's will can enter the kingdom of heaven.

59

FIFTH SUNDAY AFTER EPIPHANY

First Lesson   II Kings 4.18–21, 32–37

From the Old Testament we hear **the story of the prophet Elisha bringing new life to the son of a Shunammite woman.** The woman bore a son as Elisha had prophesied. When, however, the grown child died, Elisha did not learn of it until the woman came to him. He then restored the young man to life and returned him to his mother. Such is the power of the Lord acting through God's prophet.

Psalm 142: A lament and a cry to the Lord for help.

Second Lesson (The Epistle)   I Corinthians 9.16–23

In this reading we learn how **Paul seeks to become all things to all people in order that he may freely and without hindrance share the gospel with them.** He takes no special pride in his preaching of the gospel because that is his commission from the Lord. In order not to create unnecessary difficulties, he is willing to live under the law among Jews and outside the law among Gentiles. Some may misunderstand and think him unprincipled, but Paul's only concern is with the essentials of the gospel.

The Gospel   Mark 1.29–39

Our Gospel tells of **healing events which took place toward the beginning of Jesus' ministry.** Peter's mother-in-law is cured of a fever. Many flock to Jesus. He heals them and casts out the demons who recognize him for who he is. A brief retreat ends because of the pressing need to continue his mission. The power of the reign of God is made manifest through his words and deeds.

The Old Testament lesson may be extended by reading all of II Kings 4.8–37, for which the introduction above will also be appropriate. The shorter version begun at verse 18 needs a more complete opening phrase, such as "When the child of the Shunammite woman had grown, . . ."

FIFTH SUNDAY AFTER EPIPHANY

First Lesson   Judges 6.11–24a

Our Old Testament lesson tells of **the calling of Gideon to deliver Israel from the Midianites.** As so often in the Bible, the Lord chooses one who seems insignificant in human sight. Gideon himself at first doubts, but through his angel the Lord promises to be with him. A sign is given to show that this is indeed the Lord's messenger.

Psalm 85 (or 85.7–13): The psalm both celebrates and prays for the Lord's gracious favor, God's forgiveness, deliverance and justice.

Second Lesson (The Epistle)   I Corinthians 15.1–11

Paul reminds the Corinthians of his basic proclamation concerning the Lord's resurrection. All these things happened according to the scriptures. Beginning with a manifestation to Cephas, Paul recounts six appearances of the risen Lord to his followers. The last, which must have taken place several years after the others, gave this former persecutor of the church his commission as an apostle.

The Gospel   Luke 5.1–11

Our Gospel is **the story of the calling of Simon Peter, together with the brothers James and John, to be disciples of Jesus.** This happens by the Lake of Gennesaret or Galilee. Jesus amazes Peter by showing him where he can catch a great haul of fish. Peter pours out his feelings of unworthiness, but from now on, Jesus tells him, he will be catching people.

SIXTH SUNDAY AFTER EPIPHANY

First Lesson   Ecclesiasticus 15.11–20

Our first lesson is **an instruction in the responsibility of human beings for their own actions.** The reading comes from Ecclesiasticus, otherwise known as the Wisdom of Jesus, Son of Sirach, a book composed about two centuries before the birth of Christ. The author reproves any tendency to say, "The Lord made me sin." God gives individuals a choice between good and evil.

Psalm 119.1–16 (or 9–16): The psalmist takes great delight in the Lord's statutes and seeks to keep God's commandments.

Second Lesson (The Epistle)   I Corinthians 3.1–9

In this reading **Paul admonishes the Corinthians for their bickering and divisions.** Missionaries like Paul and Apollos are not to be regarded as leaders of separate sects. They are co-workers in the Lord's field, while it is God who supplies the growth. To think otherwise is immature and is based on worldly rather than spiritual understandings.

The Gospel   Matthew 5.21–24, 27–30, 33–37

In our Gospel we hear of **Jesus' concern with the heart of human behavior.** Discipleship means far more than observance of the outward forms of the law. Genuinely to fulfill the commandments not to kill, not to commit adultery and not to swear falsely requires a transformation of one's life. One must be willing to cast away any part of the self which opposes this change of mind and heart.

SIXTH SUNDAY AFTER EPIPHANY

First Lesson   II Kings 5.1–15ab

Our Old Testament reading is **the story of the cure of Naaman from his leprosy.** Naaman, commander of the army of Syria, learns there is a prophet in Israel who might bring about his healing. The King of Israel regards the request for help as a trick in a plot to cause a quarrel. Naaman himself at first refuses to trust in what the prophet Elisha tells him to do, but then he is made clean and knows there is no god on earth except in Israel.

Psalm 42 (or 42.1–7): The psalmist laments inability to come to the house of God and thirsts for the presence of the Lord.

Second Lesson (The Epistle)   I Corinthians 9.24–27

In this lesson **Paul emphasizes the importance of self-discipline in the life of a Christian.** He had been instructing the Corinthians in the freedom disciples find in Christ. This freedom brings great responsibility and, to be effective, demands the exercise of self-control. Paul uses the analogy of the athlete who freely engages in a strict regimen of discipline in order to obtain the prize.

The Gospel   Mark 1.40–45

Our Gospel tells of **the healing of a leper by Jesus and the fame which follows him.** Since leprosy was a disfiguring illness which caused people to be rejected, and was often considered the result of sin, it was an especially dreaded disease. The evangelist indicates that Jesus wished to keep such healings quiet, perhaps to avoid misunderstandings about his ministry. In addition to charging the leper to keep silence, Jesus requires him to fulfill the levitical law in response to his cure.

SIXTH SUNDAY AFTER EPIPHANY

First Lesson   Jeremiah 17.5–10

In our lesson from the Old Testament **the prophet urges each individual to trust solely in the Lord who alone can search out human motivations.** Jeremiah's primary concern is that people should realize the importance of their choice. Only one who recognizes the powers of human self-deception and rests in the Lord can live a fruitful life.

Psalm 1: The Lord makes fruitful the lives of those who choose the way of righteousness.

Second Lesson (The Epistle)   I Corinthians 15.12–20

In this reading **Paul insists that belief in resurrection from death is basic to the faith that Jesus was raised, which, in turn, is vital to all Christian hope and experience.** If, as some suggest, there is no resurrection, then there is no reason to believe that God raised Jesus. If Jesus was not raised, then we remain in our unforgiven condition and are without hope for ourselves. In fact, however, Christ was raised and is the first of many who will find new life.

The Gospel   Luke 6.17–26

In our Gospel passage **Jesus heals many of their illnesses and teaches his disciples that the values of the kingdom of God are quite different from worldly standards.** His words offer both comfort and challenge. Those who now are poor, hungry, sorrowful and persecuted will find blessing, while the rich, satisfied and well spoken of will experience emptiness. Jesus' disciples must learn to share in material and spiritual deprivation in the world if they are to know the joy of the kingdom.

SEVENTH SUNDAY AFTER EPIPHANY

First Lesson   Leviticus 19.1–2, 9–18

In our Old Testament reading **the people of Israel are called to lives of justice and love—to be holy because the Lord their God is holy.** The goal for the behavior of God's people is nothing less than the very highest. As God's chosen ones, they are to care for the poor and weak and to avoid any form of oppression. One is to love one's neighbor as oneself.

Psalm 71 (or 71.16–24): Despite troubles and adversities the psalm-ist gives thanks for God's righteousness and faithfulness.

Second Lesson (The Epistle)   I Corinthians 3.10–11, 16–23

In this passage **Paul reminds the Corinthians that they are God's temple for which there is no other foundation than Jesus Christ.** Paul continues to deal with the problem of divisions within the Corinthian church. These new disciples must not attempt to live by the standards of worldly wisdom and say that they belong to Paul or Apollos or Cephas. The church lives by a deeper wisdom in which all things are for the Corinthians' benefit, while they them-selves belong to Christ, and Christ to God.

The Gospel   Matthew 5.38–48

In our Gospel lesson **Jesus calls his followers to a way of life that reaches far beyond worldly standards of goodness—towards the limitless excellence of their heavenly Father.** Legalistic religion has traditionally been used to define the ways in which people can limit the extent of their care for others and still regard themselves as good. Jesus presents a standard which ends all such standards. When tempted to revenge and to circumscribe love, we must seek to be like God who cares equally for all.

SEVENTH SUNDAY AFTER EPIPHANY

First Lesson   Isaiah 43.18–25

In our Old Testament reading **the Lord promises to forgive the sins of the people and to bring them back from exile through the wilderness.** The same Lord who delivered Israel through the sea and out of Egypt will do a new thing in this day. A safe way will be made in the desert. Despite Israel's iniquities and neglect of the law, God will restore them.

Psalm 32 (or 32.1–8): A psalm of thanksgiving for the forgiveness of sin.

Second Lesson (The Epistle)   II Corinthians 1.18–22

In this lesson **Paul maintains that his teaching to the Corinthians has been consistent and affirmative, based as it is in Jesus and in God's own promises.** Paul has had some difficult times with the Corinthians. They had accused him of wavering and being overly critical. Paul insists that his word has always been a positive **yes** among those who have been sealed by God and given the Holy Spirit as a kind of down-payment—a guarantee of salvation.

The Gospel   Mark 2.1–12

Our Gospel tells **the story of the healing of the paralyzed man and the forgiveness of his sins.** The press of the crowd forced the man's friends to a desperate and dramatic act in order to bring him to Jesus. The healing is a proof to the critical bystanders that Jesus, acting as the Son of Man, has authority to make known the forgiveness of sins. We may also understand the story to illustrate the bond that often exists between spiritual and physical infirmity and healing.

SEVENTH SUNDAY AFTER EPIPHANY

First Lesson   Genesis 45.3–11, 21–28

Our Old Testament lesson relates **a decisive moment in the story of Joseph as he reveals himself to his brothers, who then journey home to tell their father Jacob that his son is still alive.** The brothers are at first overwhelmed by the discovery that the brother they had sold into slavery is now Pharaoh's right-hand officer. Joseph tells them not to be upset: this has all been part of God's plan to preserve Israel during the coming time of famine.

Psalm 37.1–18 (or 3–10): A psalm of advice to the wise, instructing them to avoid evil and to wait patiently on the Lord in righteousness.

Second Lesson (The Epistle)   I Corinthians 15.35–38, 42–50

In this passage **Paul continues to discuss the question of resurrection from death.** Some of the Corinthians are not sure whether they believe in resurrection, especially if it involves a physical body. There will be some form of body, Paul tells them. In this sense individuality will continue, but it will be a body of a transformed nature. As we have lived in a body like that of the earthly Adam, so we will have a body like that of the heavenly Jesus.

The Gospel   Luke 6.27–38

In our Gospel reading **Jesus calls his followers to a way of life that reaches beyond worldly understandings of what is good.** In acts of mercy and kindness disciples are to show forth the character of their heavenly Father. This manner of love extends even to enemies. It means learning to forgive and not judging others, for the measure given will be the measure dealt in return.

EIGHTH SUNDAY AFTER EPIPHANY

First Lesson   Isaiah 49.8–18

In our Old Testament reading we hear **a prophecy of the glorious return of Israel from its exile.** The Lord will bring the people safely through the wilderness. Mount Zion in the holy city of Jerusalem may for a time consider herself forsaken; but she is the Lord's own. God would no more forget Zion than a mother would forget her child.

Psalm 62 (or 62.6–14): God is a rock and shelter. The people are to trust in God alone.

Second Lesson (The Epistle)   I Corinthians 4.1–5, 8–13

In this New Testament lesson **Paul lets the Corinthians know what it really means to be a servant of Christ.** Although Paul recognizes that only the Lord can judge his stewardship, he is obviously upset by the attitude of the new converts. In words coated with irony and sarcasm he compares their understanding of what it means to be a Christian with his own experience. If discipleship brings riches and wisdom, it does so, Paul suggests, in terms quite different from a worldly understanding of them.

The Gospel   Matthew 6.24–34

In our Gospel **Jesus urges his followers to give their allegiance to God alone and not to be anxious about life's necessities.** There are no two ways; a fundamental decision must be made between worshiping God or Mammon, the god of money. Individuals who trust in God need have no anxious worry about the material goods of life. Those who put their faith in God's reign will find they have all they need.

The lesson from I Corinthians 4 may be lengthened by including verses 6–7. The introduction above is also suitable for the longer reading.

EIGHTH SUNDAY AFTER EPIPHANY

First Lesson   Hosea 2.14–23

In this reading **the prophet pictures the Lord as wooing back his harlot wife, Israel, after which there will be a time of peace and fertility in the land.** Hosea uses a touching analogy from his own experience of marriage to suggest the character of God's love for God's people. Despite Israel's idolatry, the Lord will go out with her into the wilderness to court her into a new relationship of love.

Psalm 103 (or 103.1–6): A hymn of blessing in thanksgiving for healing forgiveness and for all the Lord's acts of compassion and justice.

Second Lesson (The Epistle)   II Corinthians 3.17–4.2

Where the Spirit of the Lord is, Paul writes, freedom is experienced, and disciples are enabled to reflect the Lord's glory. Entrusted with this commission, Paul does not lose heart, but conducts his ministry openly and honestly. The apostle had earlier explained to the Corinthians that the law of Moses brings death and, unless understood from a Christian perspective, is veiled in the same way Moses had to veil the brightness of his face after talking with God. But the Spirit of the Lord removes the veil and brings life and liberty.

The Gospel   Mark 2.18–22

In our Gospel we hear how **Jesus' presence and message have brought newness and joy into the lives of his disciples.** The disciples of John the Baptist and the Pharisees fast, but Jesus' followers do not fast because the present time may be compared to a wedding feast. Like a new wine a new spirit is present which demands a new way of life. A somber note is introduced when it is recognized that there will be a day when the bridegroom, Jesus, is taken away.

II Corinthians 3.4–11, 17–4.2 may be used for a longer second lesson. For its introduction see p. 206.

Year C

EIGHTH SUNDAY AFTER EPIPHANY

First Lesson   Jeremiah 7.1–7

In this Old Testament lesson **Jeremiah speaks the word of the Lord and calls the people to repentance and amendment of life.** All too easily do the worshipers come to the temple with pious phrases on their lips, as though just being in the Lord's house made them holy. God requires justice and an end to idolatry and oppression.

Psalm 92 (or 92.1–5, 11–14): A psalm of thanksgiving and praise. Those who choose righteousness are like a great tree planted in the house of the Lord.

Second Lesson (The Epistle)   I Corinthians 15.50–58

In this passage **Paul concludes his teaching to the Corinthians concerning resurrection from death.** Some of the new disciples either doubted the resurrection or held that Christians could already live a fully resurrected life of the spirit without any regard for the body. Paul has taught them that in the age to come disciples will have a new and changed form of life, the mortal having put on immortality. This is the promised victory over sin and death.

The Gospel   Luke 6.39–49

In the Gospel reading **Jesus presents a series of teachings concerning discipleship which is genuine at heart.** His followers are to deal with their own sins before they can see clearly to help others. It is not enough just to call on Jesus as Lord. Truly to hear his words and to do them is to be like the man who built his house on a foundation of rock.

The Old Testament lection may be expanded to include Jeremiah 7.8–15, in which case this sentence should be added to the introduction above: "Unless this happens, the temple in Jerusalem will be destroyed as was the sanctuary in Shiloh."

LAST SUNDAY AFTER EPIPHANY

First Lesson   Exodus 24.12, 15–18

In the Old Testament lesson **Moses is called up to Mount Sinai, and the glory of the Lord appears.** There he is to receive the commandments written on stone tablets. The Lord's presence is essentially indescribable, but it is known in the cloud and fire. The cloud both hides and reveals the Lord's glory, and the scene suggests the awesome majesty of a volcanic mountain.

Psalm 99: The holy and mighty Lord reigns on high. God spoke to Israel's leaders from a pillar of cloud and has forgiven them their misdeeds.

Second Lesson (The Epistle)   Philippians 3.7–14

Nothing matters, Paul writes, in comparison with knowing Christ Jesus as his Lord. If righteousness were to be based on a legalistic understanding of religion, Paul had any number of points in his favor. But all such privilege he now counts as garbage so that he may belong to Christ through faith and share in his sufferings. Forgetting what lies behind, he presses on toward the call ahead.

The Gospel   Matthew 17.1–9

Our Gospel is **the story of Jesus' transfiguration.** The narrative is richly woven with themes and symbols drawn from Israel's past and its hopes for the future. Moses and Elijah represent the law and the prophets, whose promises Jesus fulfills. Reflected in Jesus' human person chosen disciples see divine glory. They hear a voice from the cloud declaring that he is the beloved Son.

The Old Testament lesson may be expanded to include Exodus 24.13–14. The introduction above is suitable for the longer reading.

LAST SUNDAY AFTER EPIPHANY

First Lesson   I Kings 19.9–18

The reading from the Old Testament tells how **God is made known to Elijah—not in wind, earthquake or fire—but in a still small voice.** In a mood of depression the prophet retreats to Mount Horeb. But the Lord gives him a new mission and a promise that there will be a remnant in Israel who will not worship the false god Baal. Although God is known in a word of revelation rather than in the awesome events of nature, these happenings can also be seen as harbingers of God's presence.

Psalm 27 (or 27.5–11): The psalmist expresses great trust and confidence in the Lord and asks always to be in God's presence.

Second Lesson (The Epistle)   II Peter 1.16–19

This lesson presents **the apostle Peter** as he **recalls his vision of Jesus in majesty on the holy mountain and the heavenly voice which announced that this was God's beloved Son.** Peter was among those who were eyewitnesses to this revelation.

The Gospel   Mark 9.2–9

Our Gospel is **the story of Jesus' transfiguration.** The narrative draws upon themes and symbols from Israel's past and its hopes for the future. Moses and Elijah represent the law and the prophets, whose promises Jesus fulfills. Reflected in Jesus' human person chosen disciples see divine glory. A voice from the cloud declares that he is God's beloved Son.

II Peter 1.16–19 may be expanded by continuing with verses 20–21. For an introduction to the longer lection see p. 206.

LAST SUNDAY AFTER EPIPHANY

First Lesson   Exodus 34.29–35

In our first reading we hear how **Moses' face shone after he had spoken with the Lord.** When Moses came down from Mount Sinai after again receiving the ten commandments, the people were afraid to approach him because of the radiance of his face. Whenever he talked with the people, he had to wear a veil.

Psalm 99: The holy and mighty Lord reigns on high. God spoke to Israel's leaders from a pillar of cloud and has forgiven them their misdeeds.

Second Lesson (The Epistle)   I Corinthians 12.27–13.13

In this lesson **Paul teaches that, with their different gifts, all are members of the body of Christ. Yet without love, nothing one does is of any worth.** The new converts at Corinth were tempted to pride themselves on their spiritual gifts. But the most excellent way, which will endure after all other gifts have passed away, is love.

The Gospel   Luke 9.28–36

Our Gospel is **the story of Jesus' transfiguration.** The narrative is richly woven with themes and symbols drawn from Israel's past and its hopes for the future. Moses and Elijah represent the law and the prophets whose promises Jesus fulfills. While Jesus is praying, divine glory is reflected in his human person. Chosen disciples hear a voice from the cloud declaring that this is God's beloved Son.

ASH WEDNESDAY

First Lesson   Joel 2.1–2, 12–17

In our Old Testament reading **the prophet pictures the day of the Lord as a time of judgment and darkness, but he holds out the hope of mercy if the people will repent.** Some looked to the day of the Lord's coming as an event of great triumph and joy in Israel. But because of sin the sky will become black with swarms of locusts. The trumpet must be blown, calling for a solemn fast, a time for weeping, rending of hearts and turning back to a compassionate Lord.

Psalm 103 (or 103.8–14): A hymn of blessing in thanksgiving for healing forgiveness and for all the Lord's acts of compassion and justice.

Second Lesson (The Epistle)   II Corinthians 5.20b–6.10

In this lesson **Paul urges the new disciples to be reconciled to God in this time of deliverance, and he reminds them of all the hardships he has patiently endured for their sake and for the gospel.** The disciples' task is to respond to God's reconciling work in Christ who has taken upon himself their sinfulness so that they might have a right relationship with God. In order that he might offer his service without presenting any personal obstacles, Paul has accepted many of the paradoxes that were part of Jesus' own ministry. Although himself poor, he brings true riches to many.

The Gospel   Matthew 6.1–6, 16–21

In our Gospel **Jesus describes genuine charity, prayer and fasting.** For religious people the temptation is always strong to want to be recognized as full of piety more than to want honestly to be seeking God and the good of others. Praise and rewards for an outward show of religion all pass away. The real treasure is found in our relationship with God.

Isaiah 58.1–12 is an alternative first lesson. For its introduction see p. 207.

FIRST SUNDAY IN LENT

First Lesson   Genesis 2.4b–9, 15–17, 25–3.7

From the Old Testament we hear **the story of the creation of the first man and woman in the Garden of Eden and their disobedience and consequent loss of innocence.** Tempted by the serpent, first the woman and then the man eat from the forbidden tree of the knowledge of good and evil. The story expresses the understanding that human beings are the crown of God's creation, and yet there is something tragically wrong with them. From later Christian perspective, however, this transgression is seen as part of God's greater plan for the maturity and salvation of humanity. The free choice of disobedience and the learning of good and evil will, through redemption, make possible a more profound relationship with God.

Psalm 51 (or 51.1–13): A confession of sin and guilt and a prayer for a clean heart.

Second Lesson (The Epistle)   Romans 5.12–19

In this lesson **Paul tells how the history of human sinfulness and death has been transformed by the free gift of Jesus Christ.** The act of disobedience of one person, Adam, began the reign of sin and death. This was later compounded by the role of law which, by instructing people not to sin, actually caused trespassing to abound. But now the righteousness and obedience of one person, Jesus Christ, means acquittal and new life for all.

The Gospel   Matthew 4.1–11

Our Gospel is **the story of the temptations of Jesus by the devil.** After his baptism Jesus is led into the wilderness and confronted with temptations which are inescapable in his ministry. He might seek to show that he is the Son of God by satisfying material needs or wielding miraculous power. Or he could seek to control allegiance through the pomp and might of a worldly kingship. But Jesus' obedience is to God's way for him.

Romans 5.12–19 may be expanded by adding verses 20–21. The introduction above remains suitable.

FIRST SUNDAY IN LENT

First Lesson   Genesis 9.8–17

Our Old Testament lesson tells of **God's promise to Noah and to future generations never again to flood all the earth.** God establishes this covenant with a sign—the rainbow that is seen in the storm clouds. This covenant is made with the whole creation. It signifies God's purpose to preserve and save the world, not to destroy it.

Psalm 25 (or 25.3–9): A prayer for forgiveness and guidance and an expression of trust in the Lord.

Second Lesson (The Epistle)   I Peter 3.18–22

This reading from the New Testament speaks of **the significance of Christ's death and resurrection. In the story of Noah's salvation a prefigurement of our own salvation through the water of baptism is perceived.** Portions of this letter are thought to have been originally composed for use in a service of baptism and Eucharist on the eve of Easter. Such a purpose would explain the association of the themes of Christ's death, baptism and his triumphal resurrection. It is uncertain who is meant by the spirits to whom Christ preached after his death, but this activity may signify God's intention for the salvation of all.

The Gospel   Mark 1.9–13

The Gospel is **the story of Jesus' baptism followed by his temptation in the wilderness by Satan.** As Jesus comes up from the water, the Holy Spirit descends like a dove and a voice from heaven tells him that he is the beloved Son. The Spirit then guides him out into the wilderness where ancient Israel also met its temptations. Here Jesus has his first encounter with Satan.

FIRST SUNDAY IN LENT

First Lesson   Deuteronomy 26.5–11

In this reading from the Old Testament **the Lord's mighty salvation of Israel from slavery in Egypt is recalled, and the people are bid to offer in thanksgiving the first fruits of their fields.** The passage presents one of Judaism's oldest summaries of its history and confessions of its faith. It is always to be remembered that it was God who made them a people, who heard and delivered them from their distress, and gave them this good land for a heritage.

Psalm 91 (or 91.9–15): A hymn of trust in the Lord. The Lord will guard and deliver the one who loves and seeks refuge with God.

Second Lesson (The Epistle)   Romans 10.8b–13

In this lesson **Paul teaches that the word of faith is a gift to us; by it we make our saving confession that Jesus is Lord and that God raised him from the dead.** Without God's grace the way of righteousness would be impossibly distant. But the faith that leads to righteousness is in our hearts and the confession of salvation is on our lips. This is true for all people, no matter what their background, who call upon the name of the Lord.

The Gospel   Luke 4.1–13

Our Gospel is **the story of the temptations of Jesus by the devil.** After his baptism Jesus is led into the wilderness and confronted with the temptations which are inescapable in his ministry. He might seek to show that he is Son of God by satisfying material needs, or he could control lives by ruling with worldly pomp and authority. Or, in what may be seen as the greatest temptation, he could direct allegiance through miraculous power. Instead Jesus three times confesses his obedience to the will of God.

The Old Testament lesson may be expanded to include Deuteronomy 26.1–4. The introduction above remains suitable.

77

SECOND SUNDAY IN LENT

First Lesson   Genesis 12.1–8

The opening lesson is **the story of God's call of Abraham (who was then known as Abram) to leave his own country and become the father of a great nation.** Trusting in the Lord, Abram and his family forsake all that is familiar to them to set out for an unknown land. In this new country they worship the Lord. This story is a major illustration of the way God acts in history by calling individuals to venture forth in faith.

Psalm 33.12–22: Joyful are the people who trust in the Lord. From heaven God sees all who dwell on the earth.

Second Lesson (The Epistle)   Romans 4.1–5, 13–17

In this passage **Paul describes Abraham as a man who through faith found a right relationship with God. He is the father of all who trust in the Lord.** Paul uses the example of Abraham as a centerpiece for his argument that righteousness with God comes through faith and not by works of the law. The promise given to Abraham and his descendants was not made because of good works or legal obedience. It rests on grace alone.

The Gospel   John 3.1–17

In our Gospel story, **Nicodemus, one of the Pharisees, comes during the night to talk with Jesus.** Nicodemus is a figure used by the evangelist to represent a type of person who wants to believe but has difficulty understanding spiritual realities. Jesus tells him that individuals cannot enter the kingdom of God unless they are born anew through water and the Spirit. The inner meaning of the passage partly turns on the fact that "born anew" can also be understood as "born from on high" and that the same Greek word means both wind and spirit. Jesus then tells Nicodemus of the Son of Man come down from heaven who will be lifted up, both on the cross to die for the world and to return to heaven in glory.

The lesson from Romans may be expanded to 4.1–17. For an introduction to the longer lection see p. 207.

SECOND SUNDAY IN LENT

First Lesson   Genesis 22.1–14

Our Old Testament reading is **the story of Abraham's willingness to sacrifice his only son Isaac in obedience to the Lord's command.** The narrative illustrates Abraham's readiness to abandon all to serve the Lord. Originally it probably also was used as a model story encouraging the substitution of animal for human sacrifices. Ancient Israel was given a better understanding of God's will.

Psalm 16 (or 16.5–11): Contentment, refuge and joy are found in the presence of the Lord who does not abandon God's faithful servant at death.

Second Lesson (The Epistle)   Romans 8.31–39

In this lesson **Paul exults because nothing can separate us from love of God who gave God's only Son for us.** No charge can be brought against the elect who are now interceded for by the same Jesus Christ who died and then was raised from the dead. Neither mortal distress nor supernatural power can cut us off from such love.

The Gospel   Mark 8.31–38

In our Gospel passage **Jesus teaches his disciples of the true nature of the ministry of the Son of Man and what it means to follow in his way.** Peter has just previously stated his belief that Jesus is the Christ. But now he is called Satan because he tempts Jesus with human ideas rather than God's. Peter needs to understand that, as the Son of Man, Jesus' mission leads through suffering and death before resurrection. Disciples must also learn that the true self and true life are found by those who let themselves be lost for the sake of Jesus and the gospel.

SECOND SUNDAY IN LENT

First Lesson   Genesis 15.1–12, 17–18

Our Old Testament lesson tells of **the promise of many descendants and of a convenant guaranteeing a homeland which God made with Abraham (who at that time was known as Abram).** Abram had no children and was planning that one of the slaves born in his house would be his heir. Now he puts his faith in God and is accepted into a right relationship with the Lord. A covenant is then established by means of an ancient custom. Animals are divided in half and, in the form of smoking and flaming symbols, God passes between them.

Psalm 27 (or 27.10–18): The psalmist expresses great trust and confidence in the Lord and asks always to be in God's presence.

Second Lesson (The Epistle)   Philippians 3.17–4.1

In this reading **Paul warns of enemies of the cross of Christ and urges the disciples in Philippi to stand firm in the hope of the glory to come.** Previously Paul has told how he had learned to count all privileges of birth and background as of no value in comparison with faith in Jesus. He asks the Philippians to imitate him, and to be wary of those who glory in material appetites and values, whether religious or otherwise. Christians are to see themselves already as citizens of heaven, expecting Christ to come and to transfigure their present bodies into the form of their Lord's own resplendent existence.

The Gospel   Luke 13.31–35

In our Gospel **Jesus is disdainful of King Herod's threat and expresses his determination to fulfill his prophetic destiny in Jerusalem.** Jesus' words emphasize his struggle against the forces of evil and illness and his expectation concerning what will soon happen to him in Jerusalem. He laments over the city, once chosen for God's temple, but which has killed so many prophets before him.

The Gospel lesson may be lengthened to include Luke 13.22–30. An introduction for this longer lection is on p. 207.

THIRD SUNDAY IN LENT

First Lesson   Exodus 17.1–7

In our Old Testament story **the people are at the point of rebellion because they are without water in the wilderness.** Moses decries their readiness to challenge the Lord through their lack of trust, and he asks God what is to be done. The Lord instructs Moses to strike a rock with his staff so that water will pour from it. This place he named Massah (meaning Challenge) and Meribah (meaning Dispute).

Psalm 95 (or 95.6–11): A call to worship the Lord our God, with a warning not to put God to the challenge.

Second Lesson (The Epistle)   Romans 5.1–11

In this reading **Paul bids disciples to rejoice in the reconcilation and hope which are theirs because of the sacrifice of Christ on behalf of sinners.** Through faith we have justification; we are given a right relationship with God. Now even our sufferings can lead to endurance, and this to a perseverance which strengthens our hope. Since God was willing to show such a love while we were still God's enemies because of sin, how much more we are assured that we are to be saved.

The Gospel   John 4.5–26, 39–42

Our Gospel tells **the story of Jesus' meeting with the Samaritan woman by Jacob's well.** The narrative is rich with themes. Jesus is willing to break with custom in order to talk with one who is both a woman and a foreigner. True worship of God is tied to no place. He himself offers a living water which wells up to eternal life. The woman learns that Jesus is the expected Messiah, and later others from the town come to believe that he is the world's Savior.

The Gospel may be expanded to include John 4.27–38, in which case to the introduction above, the following sentence may be added: "During an interval in the story, Jesus speaks with his disciples concerning his true food and drink, and tells them that the time of harvesting for eternal life is at hand."

THIRD SUNDAY IN LENT

First Lesson   Exodus 20.1–17

In our first reading **Moses gives the people the ten command-ments which God spoke to him on Mount Sinai.** These precepts are at the heart of Israel's law or torah, and form the basis of the cove-nant with God established through Moses. The first four command-ments prescribe Israel's relationship with God. Those which follow require fundamental responsibilities in human relationships.

Psalm 19.7–14: A hymn in praise of the law of the Lord together with a prayer for the avoidance of sin.

Second Lesson (The Epistle)   Romans 7.13–25

In this lesson **Paul continues to wrestle with the question of the role of the law. Although the law is good in principle, without God's saving act in Jesus, it only produces more sinfulness.** Paul feels two strong and opposing tendencies within his being. Without the new relationship of faith through Jesus, the regulations of the law only cause the tendency to break the law to grow stronger. Paul speaks of this as a tendency of his flesh, by which he means all within him that does not seek faithful obedience to God.

The Gospel   John 2.13–22

Our Gospel is **the story of Jesus' cleansing of the Jerusalem tem-ple of its commercial activities, and his prediction that his body will become the new temple.** The fourth evangelist places this incident very early in Jesus' ministry. It signifies the need to cleanse reli-gious practices of corrupting influences and to put in their place a new form of worship. In the future Christians will worship God by sharing together in the risen life of Christ.

THIRD SUNDAY IN LENT

First Lesson   Exodus 3.1–15

In our Old Testament story **Moses is encountered by the Lord in the burning bush. He is called to his mission to lead the people of Israel out of slavery in Egypt, and he asks to know the name of this God of his ancestors.** God's answer to Moses is intriguing and mysterious. The response may indicate a proper name which traditionally has been known as Yahweh. God's answer may, however, suggest a meaning like "The One who causes to be," or "I am who I am," or "I will be what I will be."

Psalm 103 (or 103.1–11): A hymn of blessing in thanksgiving for healing forgiveness and for all the Lord's acts of compassion and justice.

Second Lesson (The Epistle)   I Corinthians 10.1–13

In this reading **Paul looks back to the great events of the exodus story and sees lessons for contemporary Christians.** Some disciples apparently believed that participation in baptism and the Eucharist would automatically prevent sin and excuse them from judgment. Paul suggests that the passing of the Israelites through the sea and the food and water they received in the wilderness can be uderstood as types of the Christian sacraments. Yet the Israelites still committed sin and fell into condemnation.

The Gospel   Luke 13.1–9

In our Gospel **Jesus uses two contemporary disasters and a parable of his own to stress the need for repentance.** Some might think that those who died in these tragedies were more sinful than others. Not necessarily so. Unless people use the time allotted for a change of heart and turning to God, they too will come to a tragic end.

FOURTH SUNDAY IN LENT

First Lesson   I Samuel 16.1–13

In our Old Testament story **the Lord sends Samuel to anoint David to be the new king over Israel.** God has rejected Saul as king, but he remains in power and Samuel must go secretly on his mission. As so often happens in the Bible, one who seems least likely in the eyes of others is chosen by God to carry out the divine will.

Psalm 23: The Lord is shepherd and guide. God is present in the time of danger and is generous and merciful.

Second Lesson (The Epistle)   Ephesians 5.8–14

In this New Testament lesson **disciples are called to be a people of the light, forsaking all the works of darkness.** Their present life is to be in sharp contrast with their actions before they became Christians. All that is done is to be exposed to the light. The passage closes with what was probably part of an ancient hymn used at baptisms.

The Gospel   John 9.1–13, 28–38

Our Gospel is **the story of Jesus' healing of a man born blind. Jesus brings light into a dark world.** Many people of the time regarded the man's blindness as a result of sin, but Jesus helps him to see, at first physically, and then spiritually as well. The man withstands the criticism of the religious officials and worships Jesus as the Son of Man and his Lord.

The lesson from Ephesians may be expanded to include 5.1–7. For an introduction to the longer lection see p. 208. The Gospel reading may be expanded to include all of John 9.1–38. The introduction above is also suitable for the longer passage.

FOURTH SUNDAY IN LENT

First Lesson   II Chronicles 36.14–23

Our Old Testament reading tells how **Judah, because of its un-faithfulnes, was utterly defeated by the Chaldeans. The survivors were taken away into exile in Babylon until it was the Lord's will to restore Jerusalem through the agency of King Cyrus of Persia.** This narrative was composed by what is known as the priestly tradition of the Old Testament. The emphasis falls heavily on the lack of trust and disobedience of the leaders and priests of Judah and their heedlessness of the warnings of the prophets.

Psalm 122: A pilgrim's song of praise and prayer for the peace of Jerusalem.

Second Lesson (The Epistle)   Ephesians 2.4–10

This New Testament passage emphasizes the manner in which **Christians have been saved by God's free gift.** When we were dead in our sins, God raised us up with Christ that we might know the immeasurable riches of God's graciousness. Although we are saved by faith and not by our good deeds, we are now able to do the good works for which God has made us capable.

The Gospel   John 6.4–15

Our Gospel is **the story of the feeding of five thousand people by Jesus.** The narrative recalls the story of the food miraculously provided to the Israelites in the wilderness. So do the people declare Jesus to be the new prophet whom God had promised to raise up in Moses' place. But then they misunderstand Jesus' mission and want to make him a king because he has provided them with food. The story contains a number of other themes. The twelve baskets of fragments may signify the mission to the Gentile nations. Christians perceive in this meal a fortaste of the messianic banquet in heaven. It also prefigures the Eucharist. Jesus is the bread come down from heaven.

FOURTH SUNDAY IN LENT

First Lesson   Joshua 5.9–12

The Old Testament reading tells of **the first Passover kept by the Israelites after they had crossed over the Jordan River into the promised land.** Now that they can eat the produce of the countryside, there is no longer need for the miraculous manna of the wilderness. This happens at Gilgal, a name meaning *wheel*, which suggests the wordplay as God declares the reproaches of the people to be *rolled away*.

Psalm 34 (or 34.1–8): A hymn of blessing and praise to the Lord for God's deliverance.

Second Lesson (The Epistle)   II Corinthians 5.17–21

In this passage **Paul celebrates God's reconciling work in Christ which now makes its appeal to others through his disciples.** Those who are united to Christ are part of a new order of creation. For our sake Christ experienced the consequences of human sin that we might have a right relationship with God. Now we are ambassadors of this message of reconciliation.

The Gospel   Luke 15.11–32

Our Gospel is **the parable of the prodigal son, his elder brother and their loving father.** Hearers are meant to participate in the story by experiencing how it feels to be these individuals. One notices that the wastrel son thinks his father will only take him back if he promises to work hard and form a legalistic relationship with him. But what is the father to do when he sees his long-lost son coming down the road? How is the elder son to react to his brother's joyous welcome? The parable closes by leaving that last question to us.

The Old Testament lesson may be expanded by beginning with Joshua 4.19–24. For an introduction to the longer passage see p. 208.

FIFTH SUNDAY IN LENT

First Lesson   Ezekiel 37.1–3, 11–14

In our opening reading **the prophet has a vision of the bones of a dead and hopeless people being restored to new life in their homeland.** The Lord calls upon Ezekiel as Son of Man to prophesy that the people who have experienced exile and many hardships will live again. The Spirit of the Lord restores their spirit and breath, and they rise from death. Although this passage can be understood to anticipate the hope of individual resurrection, Israel did not yet have this belief.

Psalm 130: The psalmist calls to the merciful Lord and waits upon God for forgiveness and redemption.

Second Lesson (The Epistle)   Romans 6.16–23

This lesson teaches that **by the grace of God Christians are no longer slaves to sin but are obedient to the service of righteousness.** Paul is concluding his long discussion of the way in which disciples have been given a right relationship with God through faith. They are no longer set on a course that leads through immorality to death. To use a very human analogy, they are now slaves of righteousness and are bound to the service of God, which leads to holiness and eternal life.

The Gospel   John 11.17–44

The Gospel is **the story of Jesus' raising of Lazarus from the dead.** This is the last and greatest of Jesus' signs, and it points beyond itself to the hope of new life after death for all. Only slowly do Jesus' friends begin to understand what he is saying to them and the deeper meaning of their own words. Soon the one who has raised Lazarus will himself be put to death, and then become the way of resurrection to eternal life.

The Old Testament lesson may be expanded by including Ezekiel 37.4–10 and the Gospel, lengthened by adding John 11.1–16. The introductions above are suitable for both of the longer readings.

FIFTH SUNDAY IN LENT

First Lesson   Jeremiah 31.31–34

In our Old Testament reading **the prophet foresees a new covenant which God will make with the Lord's own people, a covenant written not on tablets of stone but on human hearts.** Israel and Judah have broken the covenant which the Lord made when he brought them out of slavery in Egypt. Now they are about to go into exile. Yet the days are coming when their sins will be forgiven, and God will establish a new relationship with them. This covenant will be based not on external law but on an inner knowing of the Lord.

Psalm 51 (or 51.11–16): A confession of sin and guilt and a prayer for a clean heart.

Second Lesson (The Epistle)   Hebrews 5.5–10

In this New Testament lesson we hear how **through his obedience and suffering Christ reached the perfection of his destiny and was designated by God to be the eternal high priest.** The high priesthood of Jesus is the great theme of the Letter to the Hebrews. Like the high priests of the old covenant, Christ is chosen from among men and so has sympathy with human weakness. But he is the Son and has now been named high priest forever. He succeeds Melchizedek, a royal and priestly figure from antiquity.

The Gospel   John 12.20–33

In this Gospel passage **Jesus presents teaching concerning the meaning of his death. After his prayer to God a voice from heaven is heard.** Greeks wish to see Jesus, but he will not draw all others to himself until after he has died and risen. Then, like a seed which falls into the earth, he will bear much fruit. Disciples must also learn to serve Jesus by following him in this way. Now is the hour for the Son of Man to be glorified—glorified both by his willingness to be lifted up on the cross to die for others, and afterward to be lifted up to heaven.

FIFTH SUNDAY IN LENT

First Lesson   Isaiah 43.16–21

Our Old Testament reading tells how the same Lord who brought the people through the Red Sea waters and crushed the army of the Egyptians will do a new thing in this day when God will bring the people home through the wilderness. No longer need the Israelites only remember the things the Lord did for them in the past. It is the end of the exile; again God forms the chosen people. A safe way will be made in the wilderness, and rivers will flow in the barren desert.

Psalm 126: A song of hope and joy sung to the Lord who restores the fortunes of God's people.

Second Lesson (The Epistle)   Philippians 3.8–14

Nothing matters, Paul writes, in comparison with knowing Christ as his Lord. If righteousness were to be based on a legalistic understanding of religion, Paul had any number of points in his favor. But all such privilege he now counts as garbage so that he may belong to Christ through faith and share in his sufferings. Forgetting what lies behind, he presses on toward the call ahead.

The Gospel   Luke 20.9–19

Our Gospel is **the parable of the wicked tenants of the vineyard.** The parable is presented as an allegory in which God is the owner of the vineyard. The tenants abuse the Lord's servants, the prophets, and then kill the son and heir when he is sent to them. Then the tenants will be destroyed, and the vineyard given to others. The parable is understood to point to the fulfilment of a prophetic oracle: the stone once rejected becomes the head of the corner; that is, the corner-stone of the new Israel.

PALM SUNDAY

The Liturgy of the Palms

Psalm 118.19–29: A festival hymn sung in procession in praise of the Lord's salvation.

Year A   Matthew 21.1–11

In this Gospel lesson **Jesus comes to the holy city of Jerusalem and is hailed as the promised Son of David.** He has a young donkey brought to him, and, as did the kings of old in royal celebrations, Jesus rides on it, while the crowds spread their garments and branches in the way and shout in his honor. The evangelist perceives this as a fulfillment of the prophet Zechariah's words concerning the coming king. Here is both great drama and irony as Jesus enters the city he would save, while the people who will soon call for his blood rumor it about that the prophet from Galilee has arrived.

Year B   Mark 11.1–11a

In this Gospel reading **Jesus approaches the holy city of Jerusalem, and his disciples sing praises to God in anticipation of the coming of a new kingdom of David.** He has a colt brought to him, and, as did the kings of old in royal celebrations, Jesus rides on it, while his followers spread their garments and leafy branches in the way and shout "Hosanna". Here is great drama as he enters the city and temple he would save, but there is also acute irony for those who know what lies ahead.

Year C   Luke 19.29–40

In this Gospel lesson **Jesus, his long journey finally over, approaches the holy city of Jerusalem, while his disciples hail him as the king who comes in the Lord's name.** He has a colt brought to him and, as did the royal figures of old, Jesus rides on it while his many followers spread their garments in the way and shout praises to God. Certain of the religious officials wish Jesus to rebuke his disciples, but on this day the very stones are ready to cry out. Here is great drama as the Lord comes to the city he would save, yet also acute irony for those who know what lies ahead.

PALM SUNDAY
The Liturgy of the Word

First Lesson   Isaiah 45.21–25

In our Old Testament reading **the prophet speaks the word of the Lord: there is no other god. The Lord alone is able to save.** As the passage opens, those who pray to other gods and idols are urged to try to make their case. But there is no other Lord of all the world. This Lord will fulfill the divine promise, and every knee will bow and all tongues witness to the Lord God.

Psalm 22.1–21 (or 1–11): A psalm of lamentation and a plea for deliverance by one who feels deserted and pressed in on every side.

Second Lesson (The Epistle)   Philippians 2.5–11

From one of the earliest Christian hymns we hear how Christ Jesus accepted the condition of a servant, was obedient even to the point of death, and was then given the name above every name. It is possible that this poem was adapted by Paul or another disciple from the hopes for a savior of a people who did not yet know Jesus. He has fulfilled humanity's dream of one who will share fully in the mortal condition before his exaltation. To him every knee shall bow and every tongue confess the great name of the Lord now known in person, Jesus.

For an introduction to the alternative first lesson, Isaiah 52.13–53.12, see the lections for Good Friday on p. 94.

PALM SUNDAY

Year A

The Gospel   Matthew 26.36–27.54 (55–66)

Our Gospel is **the story of Jesus in the Garden of Gethsemane, his trials before the Jewish Council and Pilate, followed by his final sufferings and death.**

or Matthew 27.1–54 (55–66)

Our Gospel is **the story of Jesus' trial before Pilate, his final sufferings and death.**

Year B

The Gospel   Mark 14.32–15.39 (40–47)

Our Gospel is **the story of Jesus in the Garden of Gethsemane, his trials before the Jewish Council and Pilate, followed by his final sufferings and death.**

or Mark 15.1–39 (40–47)

Our Gospel is **the story of Jesus' trial before Pilate, his final sufferings and death.**

Year C

The Gospel   Luke 22.39–23.49 (50–56)

Our Gospel is **the story of Jesus' last hours in prayer, his trials before the Jewish Council, Pilate and Herod, followed by his final sufferings and death.**

or Luke 23.1–49 (50–56)

Our Gospel is **the story of Jesus' trials before Pilate and Herod, his final sufferings and death.**

If the verses in parentheses are included, the last phrase should read: ". . . his final sufferings, death and burial."

MAUNDY THURSDAY

First Lesson   Exodus 12.1–14a

In our Old Testament lesson **instructions are given, and the meaning of the passover meal is told: it is a remembrance and re-enactment of Israel's beginnings as a people when they were saved out of slavery in Egypt.** The details indicate that several different traditions stand behind the passover memorial. Perhaps it was the Israelites' attempts to keep ancient spring rites, derived from their shepherding and agricultural backgrounds, which caused the Egyptians to persecute them. With these traditions the story of God's judgment on Egypt and victory for God's people has become richly entwined.

Psalm 78.14–20, 23–25: The psalm recalls Israel's trials and temptations in the wilderness after they had escaped from Egypt. The Lord gives them water to drink and manna to eat.

Second Lesson (The Epistle)   I Corinthians 11.23–26

In this reading **Paul recalls the tradition he received concerning the supper of the Lord on the night he was betrayed.** The apostle reminds the Corinthians, who have shown an alarming tendency to divide up into factions, of the message he first delivered to them. This meal is a remembrance and reenactment of the Lord's offering of himself and forming of the new covenant. It proclaims the Lord's saving death and looks forward to his coming.

The Gospel   John 13.1–15

Our Gospel tells how **Jesus washes his disciples' feet during his last meal with them.** This action symbolizes the love and humility of Christ in stooping down to wash those whom he loves from their sins. He also sets them an example: he has acted as their servant; so should they serve one another.

I Corinthians 11.23–26 may be lengthened by adding verses 27–32. An introduction for the longer lection is found on p. 208. Luke 22.14–30 is an alternative Gospel reading. Its introduction is on p. 209.

GOOD FRIDAY

First Lesson   Isaiah 52.13–53.12

Our opening lesson is **the poem of the Lord's servant who suffers and bears the sins of many.** The passage is the fourth and last of the "servant songs" which form a portion of the Book of Isaiah written when the exile was coming to an end. The servant is sometimes thought to be an historical individual, or is understood as an idealization of the faithful of Israel. This "man of sorrows," "despised and rejected," "wounded for our transgressions," whom the Lord at last vindicates, is perceived by Christians to be a prefigurement of Jesus.

Psalm 22.1–21 (or 1–11): A psalm of lamentation and a plea for deliverance by one who feels deserted and pressed in on every side.

Second Lesson (The Epistle)   Hebrews 10.1–25

In our New Testament reading we hear that **the way of the law has been no more than a foreshadowing of true sanctification. It calls for repeated sacrifices for sin, but Christ has offered a sacrifice for all time, and has given us a new and living way.** He has established the promised new covenant through which our sins are forgiven and God's laws are written on our hearts. Given such confidence, we are to be unswerving in our hope and strong in our encouragement of one another.

The Gospel   John 18.1–19.37

Our Gospel is **the story of Jesus' trials before the Jewish Council and Pilate, followed by his final sufferings and death.**

For the first lesson Genesis 22.1–18 or Wisdom 2.1, 12–24 may be used. See the introductions on page 209. Psalms 40.1–14 (see p. 50) or 69.1–23 (see p. 131) may serve for the psalter reading.

The Gospel passage may be shortened to John 19.1–37, in which case the following brief introduction may be used: Our Gospel is **the story of the handing over of Jesus by Pontius Pilate to his final sufferings and death.**

EASTER DAY: Early Service

If this service is the Easter Vigil, all or several of the lessons from the Old Testament indicated in the Book of Common Prayer (pages 288–291) will be used. If the service be a Eucharist without the Vigil, then any of these lessons may be used for the Old Testament reading. An introduction suitable for Genesis 1.1–2.2 is on p.118; for Genesis 22.1–18, on p. 209; for Ezekiel 37.1–14, on p. 87; for Zephaniah 3.12–20, on p. 37. As the Exodus lesson is highly appropriate for the day, its introduction is given here.

First Lesson   Exodus 14.10–15.1

Our reading from the Old Testament is **the story of the deliverance of Israel from bondage in Egypt.** The people are terrified when they see the pursuing army and complain that it would have been better to live in slavery than to die in the wilderness. Moses urges them to courage, for they will see the salvation of the Lord who has called them to freedom to serve the one true God. The Lord then brings them safely through the sea and destroys the army of the Egyptians.

Psalm 114: A song of praise to the Lord who has brought the people safely out of Egypt and through the wilderness to the promised land.

Second Lesson (The Epistle)   Romans 6.3–11

In this lesson we hear that, **as Christian disciples have been joined with Christ in his death through baptism, so they are to know a resurrection like his.** In union with Christ we have died to our sinful selves and have begun to experience a new way of life. In one sense our freedom from death still awaits us in the future, but, in another sense, we already know what it means to be alive to God in Christ Jesus and to realize the true meaning of life.

The Gospel   Matthew 28.1–10

Our Gospel tells of **Jesus' resurrection.** It is about daybreak as the women come to the grave. No human eye sees Jesus rise, but there is an earthquake and an angel of the Lord rolls away the stone covering the tomb. He tells the two Marys that Jesus goes before his disciples to Galilee. With both fear and joy in their hearts, they run to tell the disciples and, on the way, are met by their risen Lord.

EASTER DAY: Principal Service

First Lesson   Acts 10.34–43

In this lesson **Peter realizes that the good news of the gospel is meant for all people, and he proclaims the crucified and risen Jesus.** At first Peter was slow to believe that God wanted him to bring the word to a non-Jew. But God has shown this to be the divine will, and Peter gladly responds to Cornelius, a Roman centurion, together with his family and friends. The risen Jesus has appeared to chosen witnesses, and all who trust in him receive forgiveness of sins in his name.

Psalm 118.14–29 (or 14–17, 22–24): A festival hymn sung in procession in praise of the Lord's salvation and deliverance from death.

Second Lesson (The Epistle)   Colossians 3.1–4

Those who have shared in the experience of Christ's resurrection are to set their minds on the things that are above. Although disciples still live on earth in anticipation of the glory to come, in another sense they have already died to their former ways of sin. The true meaning and destiny of their lives is hidden with Christ in God.

The Gospel   John 20.1–10

Our Gospel tells of **the discovery of the empty tomb.** While it is still dark, Mary Magdalene comes and finds that the stone used to cover the tomb has been moved away. She runs and brings Peter and another disciple whom Jesus loved. Although no human eye catches sight of Jesus' rising from death, these first witnesses see the discarded grave wrappings, and the other disciples perceive and believe.

Exodus 14.10–14, 21–25; 15.20–21 may be used as the first lesson, for which the introduction for Exodus 14.10–15.1 is suitable. See above at the early service. Acts 10.34–43 may then be used as the second lesson.

A longer Gospel reading is John 20.1–18. For its introduction confer p. 210. Matthew 28.1–10 is an alternative Gospel lection. See above at the early service.

EASTER DAY: Principal Service

For both years B and C Acts 10.34–43 may be used as the first or the second lesson. Colossians 3.1–4 may serve as the second lesson, and the psalter selection is Psalm 118.14–29 (or verses 14–17, 22–24). For their introductions see Year A. Below are introductions for alternative first lessons and the Gospel readings for Years B and C.

First Lesson   Year B   Isaiah 25.6–9

Our Old Testament lesson is **a prophetic hymn envisioning the day of the Lord's salvation.** The prophet uses a rich banquet as an image for the time of festival. It takes place on the mountain of the Lord's temple, Mount Zion, where heaven and earth figuratively meet. This great feast will be for all people, and even the power of death will be overcome.

The Gospel   Year B   Mark 16.1–8

Our Gospel tells how **three women disciples first learn of Jesus' resurrection.** Coming to the tomb early in the morning, they are astounded to find its huge stone covering rolled back. A young man, in appearance like an angel, announces to them that Jesus is risen and will go before his disciples to Galilee. The event is awesome, even terrifying. The women flee from the tomb and, for at least a time, report nothing to anyone because of their fear.

First Lesson   Year C   Isaiah 51.9–11

In our Old Testament reading **the prophet calls upon the same Lord who once conquered over chaos and led Israel through the sea and out of Egypt. God will bring the people back from exile.** In ancient myth Rahab was one of the names for the watery chaos monster whom God defeated before God formed the world. Now there will be a time of new creation for God's people, an end to sorrow and the beginning of everlasting joy.

The Gospel   Year C   Luke 24.1–10

Our Gospel tells how **a group of women disciples first learn of Jesus' resurrection.** Coming early in the morning to anoint the body, they find the stone covering of the tomb rolled away and the body gone. No human eye sees Jesus rise, but now two angelic figures appear and remind the troubled and frightened women that Jesus had predicted these things would happen to him. The women then report what they have heard and seen to the apostles.

SECOND SUNDAY OF EASTER

First Lesson   Acts 2.14a, 22–32

In this lesson **Peter preaches the fundamental message of the resurrection.** The time is just after the Pentecost experience and the coming of the Holy Spirit. The author of Acts presents a picture of Peter in Jerusalem telling the news about Jesus of Nazareth. Speaking to a Jewish audience, Peter seeks to show that a passage from the psalms which promises protection from the powers of death could not have applied to King David, but instead was a prophecy about Jesus' resurrection.

Psalm 111: A song of praise to the mighty and awesome Lord who is steadfast and full of compassion.

Second Lesson (The Epistle)   1 Peter 1.3–9

This New Testament reading tells of **the new birth Christians have received through baptism which brings them a living hope through Jesus' resurrection and an imperishable inheritance.** The letter is addressed to former pagans living in the country we now know as Turkey. They have been experiencing some form of persecution. They are encouraged to regard their trials as a testing, and to think of their faith as more precious than gold, which passes purified and unharmed through fire.

The Gospel   John 20.19–31

Our Gospel presents **two appearances of the risen Lord to his disciples.** The first takes place on the very evening of the day of his resurrection. The disciples are gathered in fear, but Jesus brings them peace, gives them their mission and bestows on them the Holy Spirit. A week later, Thomas, who had been absent when Jesus first appeared and who doubted his resurrection, now knows Jesus by his wounds and worships him as his Lord and God. Future disciples will not have Jesus' physical presence, but they will be blessed in their belief.

Genesis 8.6–16; 9.8–16 may serve as the first lesson. For its introduction see p. 210. Acts 2.14a, 22–32 may then be used as the second lesson. Psalm 118.19–24 is an alternative psalter selection. See Year B.

SECOND SUNDAY OF EASTER

First Lesson   Acts 3.12a, 13–15, 17–26

Peter has just healed a crippled man, and, in this passage, **he proclaims the fundamentals of the gospel to those who come running to hear him.** From the beginning the new faith showed its power through such healings, and these occasions were used for preaching the good news. Many of these speeches are presented as summaries of basic themes. The role of the apostles as witnesses to Jesus' resurrection is stressed, as is the theme of scriptural fulfillment. Here Jesus is portrayed as the great new prophet promised by Moses.

Psalm 118.19–24: A festival hymn sung in procession in praise of the Lord's salvation.

The Second Lesson (The Epistle)   1 John 5.1–6

In this lesson we hear that **belief in Jesus as the Christ, together with love of all God's children, form the heart of the Christian faith. This faith is victorious over the world: that is, over godless society.** To love God means to obey his commandments, and the essence of the commandments is the love of all who are of God. The one who overcomes the world believes that Jesus is the Son of God, who was present in the world not only through the water of his baptism but in the blood of his crucifixion.

The Gospel   John 20.19–31

Our Gospel presents **two appearances of the risen Lord to his disciples.** The first takes place on the very evening of the day of his resurrection. The disciples are gathered in fear, but Jesus brings them peace, gives them their mission and bestows on them the Holy Spirit. A week later, Thomas, who had been absent when Jesus first appeared and who doubted his resurrection, now knows Jesus by his wounds and worships him as his Lord and God. Future disciples will not have Jesus' physical presence, but they will be blessed in their belief.

Isaiah 26.2–9, 19 is an alternative first lesson. See p. 210. The Acts passage may then serve as the second lesson. Psalm 111 may be used for the psalter selection. See Year A.

THE SECOND SUNDAY OF EASTER

First Lesson   Acts 5.12a, 17–22, 25–29

In this reading from the story of the first Christians we are told how **the apostles are freed from prison and boldly continue to teach about the new Christian life.** Soon after the resurrection, the witnessing and healing work of the disciples causes their arrest. Set at liberty by the Lord's angel, they persist in their missionary activity despite being challenged again by the religious officials. Their obedience is to God alone.

Psalm 111: This psalm is an outpouring of praise for the majesty and graciousness of the Lord who redeems the people of God.

The Gospel   Revelation 1.9–19

This lesson tells of **a vision of the risen and resplendent Lord to a disciple named John, and the command given to record this and other visions in a book addressed to seven churches.** John is on an island, sent there by God or perhaps banished because of persecution. Jesus is seen in mystic glory and described like the divine figure who had appeared earlier in a dream to the prophet Daniel. Having died and returned to life, he holds power over death and hell.

The Gospel   John 20.19–31

Our Gospel presents **two appearances of the risen Lord to his disciples.** The first takes place on the very evening of the day of his resurrection. The disciples are gathered in fear, but Jesus brings them peace, gives them their mission and bestows on them the Holy Spirit. A week later, Thomas, who had been absent when Jesus first appeared and who doubted his resurrection, now knows Jesus by his wounds and worships him as his Lord and God. Future disciples will not have Jesus' physical presence, but they will be blessed in their belief.

As an alternative first lesson Job 42.1–6 may be used. For its introduction see p. 211. The lesson from Acts may then serve as the second lesson. For an introduction to the longer alternative reading, Revelation 1.1–19, see p. 211. For an alternative psalter reading, 118.19–24, see above for this Sunday in Year B.

THIRD SUNDAY OF EASTER

First Lesson   Acts 2.14a, 36–47

This reading is **a summary of the preaching and other activities of the early Christian community in Jerusalem.** The crucified one, Jesus, has been made Lord and Christ. Now is the time for repentance, forgiveness and the gift of the Spirit. There are many signs and healings as the church grows. The new disciples share fully with one another and meet for teaching, eucharistic meals and prayers.

Psalm 116 (or 116.10–17): An offering of thanksgiving and praise by one who has been rescued from death.

Second Lesson (The Epistle)   1 Peter 1.17–23

In this New Testament lesson we hear that **the price of Christian freedom from the old ways of futility has been paid with the sacrificial blood of Christ. Although now we await the judgment of God in awe, we have the faith and hope of people who have been born anew.** The letter from which this passage comes was addressed to former pagans, and may first have been read at an Easter baptismal service. Having been purified by Christ's imperishable offering, disciples are now to love one another from the heart.

The Gospel   Luke 24.13–35

Our Gospel is **the story of how two disciples were met by a stranger on the road to Emmaus. That evening, as he breaks bread with them, they know the stranger to be Jesus.** While they are walking together, Jesus interprets the scriptures to them, showing that it was necessary that Christ should suffer. Later he disappears from their sight. While their Lord is no longer physically present, the church now knows that Jesus will disclose himself in scripture and the breaking of bread, and sometimes through a stranger.

Isaiah 43.1–12 may serve as the first lesson. For its introduction see p. 211. The Acts reading may then be used as the second lesson. The Gospel would best begin, "On that same day two of Jesus' followers were going . . ."

THIRD SUNDAY OF EASTER

First Lesson   Acts 4.5–12

In this New Testament story **Peter and John, having cured a crippled man, are called to account before the high Jewish Council. Peter testifies that the source of their healing power is the same Jesus whom the leaders rejected.** Referring to scripture, Peter speaks of the stone rejected by the builders, which is nevertheless meant to be the cornerstone of the new faith. Evidently there were a number of encounters like this in the life of the early church, but the disciples continued to heal and to preach in Jesus' name.

Psalm 98 (or 98.1–5): A song of thanksgiving and praise to the victorious Lord who has made divine righteousness known and shown faithfulness to the people of God.

Second Lesson (The Epistle)   1 John 1.1–2.2

The theme of this passage is the word of life by which Christians are called to walk in the light of God. Confessing their sins, they and all others can find forgiveness through Jesus. The beginning of this letter leaves open the possibility that the *word* may be understood as Jesus himself, or Jesus as he is revealed in scripture, or in the bread of the Eucharist. When his followers share a common life in the light that is God, they can be free to be honest about their sins and then be cleansed from them.

The Gospel   Luke 24.36b–48

In our Gospel **the risen Jesus shows himself again to his disciples, and he interprets to them the scriptures which reveal that his death and resurrection were part of God's plan.** This Jesus is no ghost or phantom (as some later interpretations of the resurrection might have suggested). His appearance is real; his friends touch him and he eats with them. Now they are to be his witnesses and to carry the message of repentance and forgiveness to all peoples.

Micah 4.1–5 may be used as the first lesson. See p. 211. Acts 4.5–12 may then serve as the second lesson.

The Gospel passage might well begin, "While the disciples were talking, Jesus . . ."

THIRD SUNDAY OF EASTER

First Lesson   Acts 9.1–19a

In this reading from the story of the early church we hear how **Paul is converted from being an enemy of the Christian way in order to become the great apostle to the non-Jewish peoples.** While he is headed toward Damascus to persecute Christians, Paul is encountered by the risen Jesus. Jesus calls him by his Jewish name, Saul, and asks why he is persecuting him by persecuting his followers. Paul is blinded by the experience, but in Damascus his sight is restored and to it is added perception of his new faith and mission.

Psalm 33 (or 33.1–11): A song of praise to the Lord who creates the world and rules with justice.

Second Lesson   Revelation 5.6–14

This lesson presents **a heavenly vision of the Lamb that was slain—a figure of Jesus.** The Lamb is given a scroll which will later be unsealed and reveal momentous events to come. First the gathered elders, then angels and then all creatures sing their praises of the Lamb. He who through his blood has offered ransom for his people now lives and is worthy of all honor and glory.

The Gospel   John 21.1–14

Our Gospel tells of **another appearance by Jesus to his disciples—this time after their return to the Sea of Tiberias or Galilee.** Several of the disciples go fishing and do not immediately recognize Jesus standing on the shore and telling them where fish may be caught. Then the disciple whom Jesus loved (perhaps intended as a model for all disciples) perceives it is the Lord. Led by the impulsive Peter they all join Jesus, bringing with them their net full with a hundred fifty-three large fish. (The significance of this number remains unknown to us.) As often in these stories, they share a meal with their risen Lord.

As an alternative first lesson Jeremiah 32.36–41 may be used. For its introduction see p. 212. The above lesson from Acts may then be used in place of the reading from Revelation.

FOURTH SUNDAY OF EASTER

First Lesson   Acts 6.1–9; 7.2a, 51–60

In this lesson we hear how **in the life of the early church it became necessary to choose certain individuals for roles of service in
the community. One of them, Stephen, proclaimed the gospel and
did miracles before he was martyred.** The passage helps us to recognize the importance of some form of organization in the Christian
community. We notice also how Stephen (and later Philip) is led by
the Holy Spirit to go beyond his initial assignments and publicly to
witness for his faith. Stephen dies with words similar to Jesus' last
prayers on his lips.

Psalm 23: The Lord is shepherd and guide. God is present in the
time of danger and is generous and merciful.

Second Lesson (The Epistle)   I Peter 2.19–25

In this reading we learn that **disciples are called to bear unde-
served suffering with patience, even as Christ has set an example
for us, so that we might die to sin and live for righteousness.** This
word is addressed primarily to those who are servants, but can well
be applied to all Christians who endure pain despite having done no
wrong. Their Lord has transformed the meaning of suffering and
through his wounds brought healing. This letter was evidently written at a time when the Christians in Asia Minor were experiencing
various forms of persecution.

The Gospel   John 10.1–10

Our Gospel presents **two related images in which Jesus is first
the shepherd in charge of the sheep and then the gate through
which the sheep enter.** These teachings are set in the context of
controversy. Jesus' words are directed against religious officials who
do not know or truly care for their people. But Jesus knows his own
sheep by name. They hear his voice and find the fullness of life.

Nehemiah 9.6–15 may be used as the first lesson. For its introduction see p. 212. The
passage from Acts may then serve as the second reading.

FOURTH SUNDAY OF EASTER

First Lesson   Acts 4.32–37

In this reading we hear of **the enthusiasm and spirit of sharing and caring for one another in the early Christian community.** The apostles continue their powerful witness to the resurrection. Greed and anxiety with regard to material possessions are overcome by grace. The author of Acts may present a somewhat idyllic picture, but there is no denying the power of the gospel to bring disciples to a profoundly new way of life.

Psalm 23: The Lord is shepherd and guide. God is present in the time of danger and is generous and merciful.

Second Lesson (The Epistle)   1 John 3.1–8

In this lesson we learn that **through the Father's love disciples are now children of God, and they no longer live in sin. Their destiny is to be like Christ.** Those who live without God do not understand what it means to be a child of God any more than they recognized Jesus. But Christians know that a dramatic change has taken place in their lives, and that the mystery of what they are fully to become still awaits them. Those who persist in sin are of the devil, but the Son of God has come to undo the devil's work.

The Gospel   John 10.11–16

In our Gospel reading we are taught that **Jesus is the good shepherd who is willing to die for his sheep.** He is not like one who has been hired to tend the sheep, and who runs away in time of danger. Rather does he know the sheep with the same intimacy that he has with the Father. Jesus has shared fully in their circumstances. Together with those who are yet to be called, there will be one flock under the one true shepherd.

A longer version of the Acts lesson is Acts 4.23–37. For its introduction see p. 212. Ezekiel 34.1–10 is an alternate first lesson (introduction on p. 213), in which case the Acts reading may serve as the second lesson.

Psalm 100 may be used instead of Psalm 23. See Year C.

Year C

FOURTH SUNDAY OF EASTER

First Lesson   Acts 13.15–16, 26–33

In the first lesson we hear how **Paul, while on an early mission-ary journey, preached to the Jews and other worshipers of God who lived in Gentile lands.** Accompanied by Barnabas, the apostle responds to an invitation to speak in the synagogue at Antioch of Pisidia, a town in the heart of the country known today as Turkey. He tells how Jesus was put to death but raised up by God. He fur-ther explains how this resurrection can be understood as a fulfill-ment of statements found in the Jewish scriptures.

Psalm 100: A song of praise and thanksgiving to the Lord who is steadfast in love and faithfulness.

Second Lesson   Revelation 7.9–17

This lesson presents **a vision of those who have survived great tribulation and now worship before the throne of God and the Lamb.** These myriad saints come from all over the world and have been purified through their own sufferings in association with the sacrifice of the Lamb. But now the Lamb (which is a figure for Jesus) will be their shepherd, and they will suffer no longer. Such a vision would be a great consolation to those undergoing persecution.

The Gospel   John 10.22–30

In our Gospel **Jesus speaks to those who are unable to come to belief in him and then tells of his sheep who belong to him forever.** Some of the Jewish people gather around Jesus in one of the areas alongside the main temple. They ask if he is the Christ; but Jesus sees that they do not believe. Yet the sheep that the Father has given can never be taken from the Father's protection, and Jesus is one with the Father.

The lesson from Acts will make best sense if begun with an introductory sentence or phrase drawn from the preceding verses: for example, "Paul and Barnabas went on the Sabbath day into the synagogue at Antioch of Pisidia." This lesson may be length-ened by adding verses 34–39 of chapter 13. The introduction above is also suitable for the longer reading.

For the first lesson, Numbers 27.12–23 may be substituted. For its introduction see p. 213. The Acts lesson may then be used as the second lesson.

106

FIFTH SUNDAY OF EASTER

First Lesson   Acts 17.1–15

This lesson recalls **Paul's missionary work and adventures as he tells the good news of the gospel in the land we know today as Greece.** These stories are meant to be illustrations of both the opposition and success that Paul found in his ministry. Together with Silas, he preaches about Jesus to the Jews living in Gentile lands and shows from the scriptures that Jesus is the Messiah. Many Jews and Gentiles become believers, but others of the Jews are jealous and cause trouble for Paul, first in Thessalonica and then in Beroea.

Psalm 66.1–11 (or 1–8): A hymn of praise and thanksgiving to God who rules in majesty and delivers the Lord's people.

Second Lesson (The Epistle)   I Peter 2.1–10

The New Testament reading presents **a series of images from the Old Testament, describing Christians as a chosen people called to God's service.** It is possible that the passage was once used during an Easter season baptismal liturgy. New-born disciples are to purify themselves and, as living stones, to join themselves to Jesus, the rejected one, who now is the cornerstone of the spiritual temple. They are the new Israel, called out of darkness into light.

The Gospel   John 14.1–14

In our Gospel passage **Jesus speaks with his disciples shortly before his passion and tells them that he is the way, the truth and the life.** He is the way because he himself is going the way of the sacrifice of his death, so to prepare a place for his disciples. In this way followers will discover the truth that Jesus so intimately reflects the character of God that those who have seen him have seen the Father. All who come to the Father through Jesus will find true life.

Deuteronomy 6.20–25 may be used as the first reading. See p. 213 for its introduction. If so used, the Acts lesson may serve as the second reading.

FIFTH SUNDAY OF EASTER

First Lesson   Acts 8.26–40

This is **the story of how Philip brought the Ethiopian eunuch to faith in Jesus.** Early Christians doubtless loved to tell and retell this narrative. It shows how a significant foreign personage, who was apparently an inquirer into Judaism, learned about Jesus and was baptized. It also illustrates the way an important passage from the Old Testament, which tells of the Lord's servant who suffered for others, was interpreted as prophecy about Jesus.

Psalm 66.1–11 (or 1–8): A hymn of praise and thanksgiving to God who rules in majesty and delivers God's people.

Second Lesson (The Epistle)   1 John 3.18–24

Here is **a summary of the Christian life: disciples are to put their trust in Jesus and care for one another with a genuine love.** This letter was written while Christians were living in difficult times. If, however, they seek to act in love, they may rest assured that God is well able to overcome their guilt. Those who are faithful and loving will know an intimacy with God confirmed by the Holy Spirit.

The Gospel   John 14.15–21

In our Gospel **Jesus promises his followers that those who love him will be guided by the Holy Spirit and will also see him.** The evangelist presents Jesus in final conversation with his followers. Soon he will be taken away from them by death, but God will send another Counselor. The world (that is, Godless society) cannot receive this Spirit of truth nor come to perceive Jesus as still living. Yet those who follow the commandments of love will find new life in intimate association with Jesus and the Father.

Deuteronomy 4.32–40 may be used as the first lesson. For its introduction see p. 213. Acts 8.26–40 may then become the second lesson. For an introduction to the longer lesson, I John 3.14–24, see p. 214.

FIFTH SUNDAY OF EASTER

First Lesson   Acts 13.44–52

This reading describes how **those to whom the good news was first preached rejected the message about Jesus. The gospel was then received with joy by many non-Jewish people.** On an early missionary journey Paul and Barnabas are teaching at a synagogue in a town in the country we know today as Turkey. The harsh jealousy of a number of the Jews causes Paul to become still more strongly confirmed in his sense of ministry to Gentiles. Despite opposition Paul continues on with his work.

Psalm 145 (or 145.1–9): A hymn of praise to God for the Lord's goodness and abundant mercy from generation to generation.

Second Lesson   Revelation 19.1, 4–9

In this lesson **John, the Seer, hears great joy in heaven and foresees the majestic marriage supper of the Lamb.** Multitudes sing praises for God's saving power. The banquet of the Lamb—who is a figure for Jesus—is about to begin. Triumph over evil and suffering and the wedding of the Lamb with the saints of God are celebrated.

The Gospel   John 13.31–35

In our Gospel lesson **Jesus speaks to his disciples on the night that he is to be betrayed and handed over to death.** Yet his dying as the Son of Man will also be the way that God is glorified—both because of Jesus' sacrifice on behalf of others and because of his resurrection and victory over the power of death. Jesus' disciples will now be known by their following of his new commandment—that they love one another with the same sacrificial love he has shown them.

Leviticus 19.1–2, 9–18 may be used as an alternative first lesson, in which case Acts 13.44–52 may serve as the second lesson. For the introduction to the lesson from Leviticus see p. 65.

SIXTH SUNDAY OF EASTER

First Lesson   Acts 17.22–31

This lesson is **Paul's address in public forum to the curious citizens of Athens.** The apostle has arrived in the intellectual and cultural center of the Greek world. The author of Acts presents him delivering a kind of sample sermon for a pagan audience. Troubled by their worship of many gods, Paul uses their altar dedicated to an unknown god as an opportunity to tell them of the one true Lord of heaven and earth, and of the time of judgment and the man God raised from the dead.

Psalm 148 (or 148.7–14): The whole of creation and all peoples join together in praise of the Lord.

Second Lesson (The Epistle)   I Peter 3.8–18

This reading offers **guidance for all Christians, counseling a readiness to suffer patiently for doing what is right.** The First Letter of Peter was written at a time when Christians in Asia Minor were experiencing persecution. The author has given advice to particular groups of people and now urges all disciples to live together in love and humility, always being willing to speak in defense of their Christian hope. They should keep their consciences clear, and, if they do suffer, they are to remember how Christ, the just one, died for the unjust.

The Gospel   John 15.1–8

Our Gospel teaches that **Jesus is the true vine to which each branch must be united if it is to bear fruit.** The vine and the vineyard were well-known symbols for God's people. A living relationship with Jesus in the following of his teaching is the source of fruitful discipleship. God will cut away the dead branches and prune the healthy ones so that they will bear more abundantly.

Isaiah 41.17–20 may be used for the first lesson. For its introduction see p. 214. Acts 17.22–31 may then serve as the second lesson.

SIXTH SUNDAY OF EASTER

First Lesson   Acts 11.19–30

This lesson tells of **significant events in the life of the early church, especially the way in which Gentiles began also to believe in the Lord Jesus.** We learn that the spread of the gospel was in part the result of persecution. The city of Antioch became an important center for the new faith, and here the followers of Christ were called Christians, which may at first have been a term of abuse. Barnabas and Saul became leaders of the church in Antioch, and helped foster a close relationship with the disciples in Judea and Jerusalem.

Psalm 33 (or 33.1–8, 18–22): Joyful are those who trust in the righteous Lord who made heaven and earth.

Second Lesson (The Epistle)   1 John 4.7–21

This reading teaches that **God's love is made known to us through Jesus. In response we are to love one another.** No one has ever seen God, but to experience God's love and to recognize Jesus as God's Son is to know God. Only by not loving other humans made in God's image would we show that we do not know and love God. When we do love one another, then we live in union with God and fear is driven away.

The Gospel   John 15.9–17

In our Gospel **Jesus speaks of his great love for his disciples and calls upon them to show this same love toward each other which has come to him from the Father.** Jesus is talking with his disciples shortly before his death when he will be taken away from them. But this love has now formed his followers into a new community in relationship with Jesus and the Father. They are no longer servants but friends.

Isaiah 45.11–13, 18–19 may serve as the first lesson (introduction on p. 214), in which case Acts 11.19–30 may be used as the second lesson.

SIXTH SUNDAY OF EASTER

First Lesson   Acts 14.8–18

In this lesson we hear how **Paul heals a crippled man and then barely avoids being worshiped as a god.** Paul and Barnabas are on an early missionary venture among pagans in Asia Minor. Because of their healing work the people want to offer sacrifice to them. Hurriedly the apostles teach the Gentiles of the one, true and living God who is the creator of all things.

Psalm 67: A prayer for God's graciousness and saving power, and a bidding of praise for the Lord's justice and bounty.

Second Lesson   Revelation 21.22–22.5

In this reading **John, the Seer, presents a vision of the new Jerusalem, the paradise of God.** The city has no need of a temple or of a sun or moon, for it is enlightened by the very glory of God and the lamp of the Lamb, who is Jesus. It will be a place of purity and abundance for the saints. As in the Garden of Eden, here will be found the river and the tree of life.

The Gospel   John 14.23–29

Our Gospel tells of **Jesus' promise to his disciples of the coming of the Holy Spirit.** Although Jesus will no longer be present physically, those who continue in his love will know his abiding presence together with that of the Father. The Holy Spirit will be their counselor and bring Jesus' own words to mind. Jesus shares these things with his followers before they take place, and he gives them his peace.

As an alternative first lesson Joel 2.21–27 may be used. For its introduction see p. 215. Acts 14.8–18 may then serve as the second lesson.

All Years

ASCENSION DAY

First Lesson   Acts 1.1–11

In the opening passage of the Acts of the Apostles the author summarizes the last events and instructions of Jesus' earthly ministry before he is lifted up into heaven. The book is formally dedicated to Theophilus, who may have been an early convert to Christianity. Jesus tells his followers to wait for their baptism in the Holy Spirit, after which their missionary work will spread from Jerusalem out to all the world. Jesus will one day come again, but his disciples now have a message to bring to all peoples.

Psalm 47: A hymn of praise to the mighty king who is raised up and enthroned on high. **Or** Psalm 110.1–5: A song for the king who is called to sit and rule at the Lord's right hand.

Second Lesson (The Epistle)   Ephesians 1.15–23

In this lesson **Paul gives thanks for the faith and love of the Ephesians and prays that they may see with their inward eyes the power of God who has raised and enthroned Jesus far above all earthly and heavenly dominions.** How vast is the treasure that God offers to those who trust in God! The Lord Christ now reigns as head of the church, which is his body, and which experiences the fullness of his love.

The Gospel   Luke 24.49–53

In our Gospel **Jesus leaves his followers with the promise of the Holy Spirit and is carried up into heaven.** The disciples are to await their empowerment from on high before beginning their mission to the world. Joyfully they return from Bethany, the town where Jesus had stayed before his passion. They enter the temple and praise God.

For the first lesson there may be used Daniel 7.9–14 in Year A, Ezekiel 1.3–5a, 15–22, 26–28 in Year B, or II Kings 2.1–15 in Year C. For their introduction see pp. 198 and 215. Acts 1.1–11 may then serve as the second lesson.

Mark 16.9–15, 19–20 may be used for the Gospel. For its introductions see p. 215.

113

SEVENTH SUNDAY OF EASTER

First Lesson   Acts 1.8–14

In this reading **we hear of Jesus' promise of empowerment for mission by the Holy Spirit, after which he is envisioned being lifted up into heaven.** The author of Acts pictures the missionary work of the church spreading outward from Jerusalem. In obedience to Jesus' command, the disciples return to the city and, with others of Jesus' followers and relatives, prayerfully await the coming of the Spirit. Although Jesus will one day appear again, his community now has a ministry to bring the good news to the world.

Psalm 68.1–20: A psalm of praise to the mighty God who has brought the people out of Egypt and saved Israel from her enemies. God reigns on high.

Second Lesson (The Epistle)   1 Peter 4.12–19

In this lesson we learn that, **when Christians find it necessary to suffer for their faith, they are to know that they are sharing in Christ's sufferings.** They can even find cause for rejoicing, recognizing that this may well be a sign that God's Spirit is with them. This advice was given during an outbreak of persecution of Christians in Asia Minor. The disciples are urged to make sure that they only suffer in a right cause and are then unashamed to confess Christ's name.

The Gospel   John 17.1–11

In our Gospel **Jesus asks the Father that the glory of God may be made fully known in the Son, and he prays for his disciples through whom this glory now shines.** These words are part of what is called Jesus' high-priestly prayer offered before his death. God's glory has been shown forth in Jesus' ministry and will be radiant in his crucifixion and resurrection. Now and afterwards Jesus' followers will realize that all which Jesus has given to them has come from the Father.

Acts 1.1–14 may serve as a longer first lesson (see p. 216), or Ezekiel 39.21–29 may become the first lesson (see also p. 216), in which case either passage from Acts may be used as the second lesson. For the psalter Psalm 47 may be used. See Year B.

SEVENTH SUNDAY OF EASTER

First Lesson   Acts 1.15–26

In this lesson we hear of **the death of Judas and the selection of Matthias to take his place as one of the twelve apostles.** Peter perceives that Judas' betrayal of Jesus and his death were part of God's plan and were prefigured in the Jewish scriptures. It is also prophesied that another should replace him. This person is chosen from among those who were Jesus' companions and who can be witnesses to his resurrection.

Psalm 47: A hymn of praise to the mighty king who is raised up and enthroned on high.

Second Lesson (The Epistle)   1 John 5.9–15

In this reading **disciples are bid to believe in the testimony that God has borne to Jesus, the Son of God. They are to have confidence that their prayers are heard and that in the Son they have eternal life.** Elsewhere in this letter it is indicated that God's witness to Jesus is especially made known through the experience of love, a love made manifest in Jesus. Those who trust in Jesus as the Son of God realize this testimony within their own hearts. Refusal to accept this witness means to lose the possibility of true life.

The Gospel   John 17.11b–19

In our Gospel lesson **Jesus prays for his disciples shortly before his death, asking for their unity and sanctification in the truth.** He prays that they may be protected in the Father's *name,* that is, by God's true character as it has been made known by Jesus. Because of Jesus' revelation to them, the disciples are set apart from disbelieving worldly society. Yet, in another important sense, they remain a part of this world and are consecrated to witness to the truth in it.

Exodus 28.1–4, 9–10, 29–30 may be used as the first lesson (see p. 216), in which case Acts 1.15–26 may become the second lesson. Psalm 68.1–20 is an alternative psalter selection. See Year A or C.

SEVENTH SUNDAY OF EASTER

First Lesson   Acts 16.16–34

This reading tells of **the imprisonment of Paul and Silas after Paul had healed a slave girl who was possessed by a spirit. An earthquake opens the doors of the prison, but Paul takes the occasion to convert the jailer and his family.** This is among a series of many adventures which happened to Paul in his missionary work. It illustrates both his fortitude and the manner in which he seized every opportunity to spread the gospel.

Psalm 68.1–20: A psalm of praise to the mighty God who has brought the people out of Egypt and saved Israel from her enemies. God reigns on high.

Second Lesson   Revelation 22.12–14, 16–17, 20

In his final vision John, the seer, pictures the glorious Lord Jesus coming to judge and to save. Blessed are those who have washed their robes by sharing in the sufferings of the one who is both David's offspring and Lord. He is the brightest star of heaven. The bride, which is the church, joins with the Spirit and all others who take their part in calling, "Come!" The passage closes with one of Christianity's oldest prayers: Amen. Come Lord Jesus!

The Gospel   John 17.20–26

In our Gospel **Jesus prays for the unity of his present and future disciples with the Father and himself.** This is the closing of what has been called Jesus' high priestly prayer. The unity for which he asks reaches deeper than outward signs or human comprehension. It is the oneness of the Father's love in the Son and of the Son in the Father. This love Jesus has made known and it indwells his followers. Their unity will be a witness to the world. Jesus prays that his disciples may behold and share in the glory given to him through the Father's love before the world began.

For the first lesson I Samuel 12.19–24 may be used. See p. 217. Acts 16.16–34 may then serve as the second lesson. For the psalter Psalm 47 may be used. See Year B.

THE DAY OF PENTECOST

First Lesson   Acts 2.1–11

This lesson tells **the story of the Holy Spirit filling the apostles and empowering them to share the message of the gospel with people of different languages.** Clearly this was a most dramatic moment in the life of the early church, an experience described in terms of wind and fire. From this time forward the mighty works of God done in Jesus will be told to all the peoples of the earth, crossing barriers of language and culture.

Psalm 104.25–37 (or 25–32): The psalm describes the wonders of the world created and renewed by the Lord's Spirit. **Or** Psalm 33.12–15, 18–22: Joyful are the people who trust in the Lord. From heaven God sees all who dwell on the earth.

Second Lesson (The Epistle)   I Corinthians 12.4–13

In this reading we hear that **Christians are all of one body and are inspired by the same Spirit which is manifested in a variety of gifts and forms of service.** It is the glory of the Christian community that its members have different gifts to offer for the common good. Disciples also come from diverse backgrounds and conditions. Yet the many members form one body, and the one Holy Spirit was poured out for all to drink.

The Gospel   John 20.19–23

The Gospel describes **an appearance of the risen Lord in which he bestows the Holy Spirit on his disciples.** He brings his disciples peace and tells them of their mission. The ministry which the Father had given Jesus is now carried forward in the world by his followers. The disciples have power over the forgiveness of sins in order to guide others to repentance and faith.

For the first lesson Ezekiel 11.17–20 may be used in Year A, Isaiah 44.1–8 in Year B, and Joel 2.28–32 in Year C. For their introductions see pp. 217 and 218. Acts 2.1–11 may then serve as the second lesson. John 14.8–17 may be used for the Gospel. See p. 218.

TRINITY SUNDAY

First Lesson   Genesis 1.1–2.3

Our first lesson is **the story of creation.** As this ancient narrative opens, the Spirit of the Lord hovers like a great mother bird over the shapeless world. God then forms the heaven and the earth and all its creatures in six days. The seventh day is set aside as a day of rest. God's ultimate creative act is human life, made in the image of God, to whom rulership and responsibility over all other life are given.

Psalm 150: A song of praise and rejoicing in which all that has breath is invited to join.

Second Lesson (The Epistle)   II Corinthians 13.11–14

In this passage **Paul closes his painful letter to the Corinthians with final admonitions and words of peace and love.** There have been disagreements between Paul and his new converts. They have shown tendencies to set themselves up as superior in faith and practice to others. But Paul ends on a hopeful note, and his last words have become part of our liturgies—a way of stating the three forms of presence of the divine graciousness.

The Gospel   Matthew 28.16–20

In our Gospel reading **Jesus makes his last appearance to his disciples and gives them their mission to baptize and teach through all the world.** These words end Matthew's Gospel. His mention of doubt on the part of some of the disciples reminds us that faith has never been an easy matter. But the closing charge is an authoritative commission to bring others to faith in the name of the Father, Son and Holy Spirit.

In place of Psalm 150 Prayer Book Canticles 2 or 13 may be used. II Corinthians 13.5–14 may serve as a longer second lesson, for which the introduction above is also suitable.

TRINITY SUNDAY

First Lesson   Exodus 3.1–6

In our Old Testament story **the Lord appears to Moses in the burning bush. Moses learns that this is the same God of his ancestors, the patriarchs of Israel.** As the narrative opens, we hear that the divine figure is an angel, a messenger of God. But then Moses realizes that this is the Lord. Moses is awestruck and fearful that he will be overwhelmed in the presence of God.

Psalm 93: God reigns, the Lord of all creation. God has established the earth and subdued the great waters.

Second Lesson (The Epistle)   Romans 8.12–17

In this lesson we hear that, **if we follow our lower nature, we are enslaved and destined to death but, when we are moved by God's Spirit, we become God's children and heirs with Christ.** The Spirit makes this experience possible by prompting our lips to call upon God as Father with the same Aramaic word (Abba) that Jesus used. This new relationship means that we are no longer required to be led by baser instincts. Our heritage is life, while we must also learn to share in Christ's sufferings.

The Gospel   John 3.1–16

In our Gospel story **Nicodemus, one of the Pharisees, comes during the night to talk with Jesus.** Nicodemus is a figure used by the evangelist to represent a type of person who wants to believe but has difficulty understanding spiritual realities. Jesus tells him that individuals cannot enter the kingdom of God unless they are born anew through water and the Spirit. The inner meaning of the passage partly turns on the fact that "born anew" can also be understood as "born from on high," and that the same Greek word means both wind and spirit. Jesus then tells Nicodemus of the Son of Man come down from heaven who will be lifted up, both on the cross to die for the world and to return to heaven in glory.

In place of Psalm 93 Prayer Book Canticles 2 or 13 may be used.

TRINITY SUNDAY

First Lesson   Isaiah 6.1–8

Our first reading is **Isaiah's vision of the Lord and his prophetic commission.** The earthly temple becomes an icon for the temple in heaven. Isaiah is purged of his guilt and sin and responds to the Lord's call. The church hears in the thrice holy song of the Seraphim an anticipation of its praise of God as Father, Son and Holy Spirit.

Psalm 29: The majesty of God is described in the likeness of a mighty thunderstorm.

Second Lesson   Revelation 4.1–11

In this lesson **John, the Seer, describes his vision of worship in heaven.** Caught up by the Spirit, John beholds the magnificence of the glory of God and hears God's praise. Heavenly beings sing "Holy, Holy, Holy" to the sovereign Lord and confess the majesty of the Creator of all things.

The Gospel   John 16.12–15

In our Gospel **Jesus promises to his disciples the gift of the Holy Spirit who will guide them into all truth.** The Spirit will make known things that are to come, and will glorify Jesus in that everything declared by the Spirit will be received from Jesus. All that the Father has belongs to Jesus. The Spirit, then, reveals Jesus who himself has made the Father known.

In place of Psalm 29 Prayer Book Canticles 2 or 13 may be used. John 16.5–15 is a longer Gospel selection. For its introduction see p. 218.

THE SEASON AFTER PENTECOST

PROPER ONE
(Sunday closest to May 11)

For the introductions see the Sixth Sunday after Epiphany.

PROPER TWO
(Sunday closest to May 18)

For the introductions see the Seventh Sunday after Epiphany.

PROPER THREE
(Sunday closest to May 25)

For the introductions see the Eighth Sunday after Epiphany.

PROPER FOUR
(Sunday closest to June 1)

First Lesson   Deuteronomy 11.18–21, 26–28

In our first lesson **Moses charges the people intimately to know and faithfully to keep the commandments of the Lord.** Some Jewish people continue today to wear little boxes containing verses from the scriptures. Here Moses is pictured as speaking to the people of Israel before they enter their new land. In the manner of ancient covenants, they are promised blessings if they obey the commandments and curses if they do not and follow after other gods.

Psalm 31 (or 31.1–5, 19–24): A psalm of trust by one who looks to the Lord for mercy and protection.

Second Lesson (The Epistle)   Romans 3.21–25a, 28

In this reading **Paul teaches that the righteous God offers the gift of a right relationship to all without reference to merit according to the law.** All people, whether Jews with the law or Gentiles without it, are sinners and have no claim of their own on the holy God. Although the law is good, it cannot bring one to acceptability before God. This acceptance is God's act of graciousness accomplished through Jesus' sacrificial offering which we experience through faith.

The Gospel   Matthew 7.21–27

In our Gospel **Jesus teaches that his true followers must not just speak but do his words.** People always have a tendency to think that lip-service might be sufficient. This is especially dangerous for those who are religious and imagine that invoking the Lord's name means true worship and service. Those who do the Lord's words as well as hear them will be like one who wisely builds a house on a solid foundation.

PROPER FOUR
(Sunday closest to June 1)

First Lesson   Deuteronomy 5.6–21

In our first reading **Moses gives to the people the ten command-ments.** These precepts are at the heart of Israel's law or torah, and are the basis for the covenant with God established through Moses. The first four commandments prescribe Israel's relationship with God. Those which follow require fundamental responsibilities in human relationships.

Psalm 81 (or 81.1–10): A psalm of festival praise and an exhortation to worship the Lord alone.

Second Lesson (The Epistle)   II Corinthians 4.5–12

In this lesson **Paul teaches that, although human weakness is all too apparent in those who preach the gospel, what is proclaimed is the glorious light of the revelation of God in Jesus Christ.** The same divine light which first shone at the creation has now been mani-fested in Jesus. Human frailty becomes the means for God to prove that God alone is the source of the power of the gospel. Paul's suffer-ings and mortality are a way of sharing in the weakness and death in which Jesus himself participated. Yet, through perseverance, they point beyond themselves to the source of life greater than death.

The Gospel   Mark 2.23–28

In the Gospel **Jesus gives reason for approving his disciples' plucking grain on the sabbath day and proclaims the Son of Man to be sovereign over the sabbath law.** In this story of conflict Jesus finds a precedent in the scriptures for making room for human needs on the sabbath. Many Jewish teachers of the time agreed that the sabbath must always be seen as a blessing for human life and not as an arbitrary requirement. Jesus goes beyond this, however, in announcing that he possesses an even greater authority for human behavior than the law.

PROPER FOUR
(Sunday closest to June 1)

First Lesson   I Kings 8.22–23, 27–30, 41–43

In the Old Testament lesson **Solomon offers praise to the Lord and prays that the newly built temple may be a house for the Lord's gracious presence.** King Solomon and the elders have just given the ark of the covenant a home, placing it in the temple which they are now dedicating. Solomon recognizes that God transcends all human buildings, but asks the Lord to be present to those who call upon God in this temple—not only the people of Israel, but also foreigners who come to worship in Jerusalem.

Psalm 96 (or 96.1–9): A song to the Lord, the Creator and Ruler of all, in which the whole world is invited to join.

Second Lesson (The Epistle)   Galatians 1.1–10

In the lesson **Paul opens his letter to the Galatians with a greeting, but quickly tells them of his astonishment over what he has heard regarding their recent attitudes.** Later in the letter we learn that others have come to Galatia urging a version of the gospel which depends on certain basic observances of the Jewish law. Paul has great respect for the law, but believes it to be a perversion of God's gift in Christ to make faith dependent on any part of the law. Those who teach in this way may claim the appointment of leaders of the church, but Paul's commission is directly from Jesus and God the Father.

The Gospel   Luke 7.1–10

Our Gospel is **the story of the healing of the centurion's servant.** This narrative was important to early Christians for several reasons. As an illustration of Jesus' healing of a non-Jew, it was warrant for the mission to the Gentiles. The story is also an example of great faith, and shows how Jesus' word can heal even when he is not physically present.

PROPER FIVE
(Sunday closest to June 8)

First Lesson   Hosea 5.15–6.6

Our opening lesson is **a dialogue between God and the people: the Lord desires a faithful love and knowledge of God rather than fleeting emotions and ritual offerings.** Israel and Judah have strayed far from the Lord's service and have worshiped other gods. For this they have suffered. Now they presume that a brief repentance will restore them to God's favor.

Psalm 50 (or 50.7–15): The psalm tells of the majestic and righteous God who requires true sacrifice and thanksgiving of God's people.

Second Lesson (The Epistle)   Romans 4.13–18

In this reading **Paul explains that the new relationship with God is open to everyone who follows in the way of Abraham's faith.** This means that righteousness before God comes through God's free gift and the response of faith—not because of obedience to the law. This was first true in the case of Abraham who trusted in God's promise before the law even existed. Now it is true for all who have faith and so show themselves to be among Abraham's descendants from many nations.

The Gospel   Matthew 9.9–13

In the Gospel story **Jesus calls Matthew, the tax collector, to be his follower and acts as a friend to tax gatherers and other sinners and outcasts.** Tax collectors at this time were looked down upon as extortionists and collaborators with the occupying Roman enemy. Yet it is not those who are considered respectable who require Jesus' acceptance of them, but those who are in need of healing. Jesus remembers the prophet's words: God desires loving mercy rather than ritual observance.

PROPER FIVE
(Sunday closest to June 8)

First Lesson   Genesis 3.8–21

In our Old Testament story we hear **the results of Adam and Eve's act of disobedience in the Garden of Eden.** The narrative is richly woven with themes meant to help explain harsh features of the human condition: from pain, hard labor and death to feelings of shame about sexuality—from fear of God to estrangement from other creatures of the earth, symbolized by the serpent. By their disobedience and coming to the knowledge of good and evil the man and woman now live in disharmony with the world and even with one another.

Psalm 130: The psalmist calls to the merciful Lord and waits upon God for forgiveness and redemption.

Second Lesson (The Epistle)   II Corinthians 4.13–18

In this passage **Paul speaks of the eternal and glorious hope that belongs to Jesus' disciples even in the midst of trouble and mortality.** The apostle has just told of the difficulties which beset his ministry. These, however, have not prevented his preaching of the gospel. Now he quotes scripture to express his conviction that the belief of Christians can and must be proclaimed in all circumstances. Although our physical being is gradually decaying, we are inwardly being renewed in accordance with what is unseen and eternal.

The Gospel   Mark 3.20–35

In our Gospel lesson **Jesus is accused of being possessed by the prince of demons. He responds by describing his battle against Satan and indicating that true relationship with him is based in the doing of God's will.** The passage suggests a certain separation between Jesus and his own relatives due to the intensity of his ministry. To those who charge him with doing good by the power of evil, Jesus answers with figures of speech—one implies that Jesus himself is the man who must first bind Satan before destroying his power. A warning is given not to blaspheme against the Holy Spirit—by which perhaps is meant calling good evil.

For a longer first lesson, Genesis 3.1–21, see p. 218.

PROPER FIVE
(Sunday closest to June 8)

First Lesson   I Kings 17.17–24

In our first reading **Elijah restores to life the son of the widow of Zarephath.** A story like this was told to convey a sense of God's might and the power and special relationship of the prophet with God. Elijah had come to the house of the widowed woman because of the Lord's command, and she had shown him great hospitality. God now proves that divine power is with Elijah. The breath of life returns to the child.

Psalm 30 (or 30.1–6, 12–13): A hymn of praise and thanksgiving by one whom the Lord has saved from death.

Second Lesson (The Epistle)   Galatians 1.11–24

In this lesson **Paul reminds the Galatians that the gospel he preached to them did not come through human authority but was revealed to him by Jesus.** The apostle has just told the new converts of his astonishment at hearing how they have been willing to follow versions of the gospel said to be more official than his but which depend on obedience to aspects of the law in order to bring about a right relationship with God. Paul rehearses his conversion from dependence on his Jewish heritage and recalls his special commission to bring the good news to non-Jews. While he did later make contact with Cephas and James in Jerusalem, his understanding of the fundamentals of the gospel does not derive from human leaders.

The Gospel   Luke 7.11–17

Our Gospel is **the story of Jesus' raising to life of the son of the widow of Nain.** This narrative would have been told in the early church to emphasize the new authority over death which had been shown forth in Jesus' own resurrection. It also represents a fulfillment of Old Testament stories and prophecies and is a sign of the beginning of the new age to which the people respond with awe by glorifying God. A special feature of the account is the description of Jesus' compassion.

PROPER SIX
(Sunday closest to June 15)

First Lesson   Exodus 19.2–8a

In our Old Testament story **the people of Israel arrive at Mount Sinai after being brought out of Egypt. Through Moses the Lord offers to make covenant with them.** If they will obey God and keep the covenant, they will be to God a special chosen nation. They will become a priestly people, holy and dedicated for God's service.

Psalm 100: A call to praise and to offer thanksgiving to the Lord.

Second Lesson (The Epistle)   Romans 5.6–11

In this lesson **Paul emphasizes the trust we may have in God's reconciling love. If Christ died for us while we were still sinners and enemies of God, then we may have confidence in God's purpose of salvation for us.** Throughout this section of his letter Paul has been explaining how right relationship with God is a gift offered to us by God, not something we can earn. God did not wait for us to be good, but through the sacrifice of Jesus accepts us in order that we may turn from sin.

The Gospel   Matthew 9.35–10.8

In our Gospel reading **Jesus continues his mission of preaching, teaching and healing, and he commissions his twelve disciples in this ministry with him.** The need for this work is great. The twelve are constituted as a kind of new Israel, and their healing acts and proclamation tell that God's ruling power has drawn near. At first this ministry will be concentrated on the Jewish nation. Later it will reach to all peoples.

For an introduction to a longer Gospel lection, Matthew 9.35–10.15, see p. 219.

PROPER SIX
(Sunday closest to June 15)

First Lesson   Ezekiel 31.1–6, 10–14

In our opening reading **the prophet Ezekiel tells a parable against Pharaoh, king of Egypt.** For the moment Pharaoh may appear like the mightiest of trees—drawing nourishment from and providing protection for all the earth. In its pride this tree even reaches into the heavens. But God will cause a foreign ruler to cut it down. The parable is told to warn Israel against trusting in Egypt or any other nation for its protection.

Psalm 92 (or 92.1–4, 11–14): A psalm of thanksgiving and praise. Those who choose righteousness are like a great tree planted in the house of the Lord.

Second Lesson (The Epistle)   II Corinthians 5.1–10

In this lesson **Paul speaks of his confident hope and his longing to experience the transformed body of heavenly existence.** It will be like having a new house or set of clothes replace—or better—be put on over this tent of a body. In any case, we will not be left just as souls without form, but will have some manner of personal existence. God's Spirit is already our guarantee. This is our true destiny where we shall be at home with the Lord, and where we shall also be judged for our use of this earthly life.

The Gospel   Mark 4.26–34

In our Gospel **Jesus tells the parables of the seed growing secretly and of the mustard seed in order to suggest what the kingdom of God is like.** God's activity is often unseen and mysterious, but it will produce its fruit and bring about the time for harvest. To human eyes the beginning of the kingdom seems insignificant, but suddenly it will break forth. The great bush, which the mustard seed becomes, is a symbol for the protection of the reign of God. The evangelist closes the passage with his understanding that only faithful disciples can perceive the significance of Jesus' parables.

PROPER SIX
(Sunday closest to June 15)

First Lesson   II Samuel 11.26–12.10, 13–15

This reading is **the conclusion of the sorry tale of David's adultery with Bathsheba whose husband Uriah was led to his death in battle at David's command.** David has acted miserably and then lowered the shades of his conscience. The Lord sends the prophet Nathan and, by means of a story, he finds a way to catch the conscience of the king. David is granted forgiveness and will not die for his crime, but will suffer through the death of his child.

Psalm 32 or (32.1–8): A thanksgiving for the forgiveness of sin.

Second Lesson (The Epistle)   Galatians 2.11–21

In this lesson **Paul tells of his dispute with Cephas and insists that justification with God cannot come through food regulations or any other laws.** Cephas, whose other name is Peter, had apparently first agreed to eat with Gentile Christians without requiring that they observe certain Jewish food laws. Later, however, under criticism from stricter Jewish Christians, he withdrew from this fellowship. That kind of dependence on the law, Paul argues, is over and done with. The only life that matters is found with Christ.

The Gospel   Luke 7.36–50

Our Gospel is **the story of Jesus' association with a woman known as a sinner and his teaching on the significance of generous forgiveness.** As at other times, Jesus is criticized for his willingness to relate to an individual regarded as a sinner. He allows the woman to demonstrate her repentance and scandalizes those present by telling her that her sins are forgiven. Much forgiveness and much love are closely linked together.

PROPER SEVEN
(Sunday closest to June 22)

First Lesson   Jeremiah 20.7–13

In our Old Testament lesson **Jeremiah complains to the Lord. He is torn between wanting to give up his mission and his need to speak in God's name and to put his trust in God.** Jeremiah has been given a most difficult ministry. In the period shortly before the final defeat of Judah and its time of exile all he can do is prophesy violence and destruction as God's judgment on the people. Even his so-called friends persecute him. Yet the Lord is on his side.

Psalm 69.1–18 (or 69.7–10, 16–18): An individual who is sunk in distress and reproach calls upon the Lord for rescue.

Second Lesson (The Epistle)   Romans 5.15b–19

In this reading **Paul contrasts the consequences of Adam's disobedience and sin with the results of Jesus' obedience and righteousness.** The effects of one individuals transgression has meant that all his descendants have found themselves in a condition leading to condemnation and death. This pattern has been transformed because of God's free gift through another human life, that of Jesus Christ. Now acquittal and a right relationship with God are available in abundant measure.

The Gospel   Matthew 10.24–33

In our Gospel **Jesus warns his disciples of troubles to come, but offers them assurance of the Father's care and his own readiness to support them before God as they speak up for him.** Because they are Jesus' disciples, people will do to them what they did to him. Just as they called Jesus Beelzebub (or the devil), so they will charge his followers. But the disciples are not to be afraid. Everything must be made known. The body may be destroyed, but not the soul which trusts in God.

In the lesson from Romans it will be helpful to identify the one man as Adam in the opening phrase. For a longer version of the Gospel, Matthew 10.16–33, see p. 219.

PROPER SEVEN
(Sunday closest to June 22)

First Lesson   Job 38.1–11, 16–18

In our first reading **God appears to Job out of the whirlwind and demands to know whether he is wise enough to question the Creator of the heavens and earth.** The challenge seems almost brutal. Job, out of all his distress, had complained about the unfairness of life. He is now forced to recognize how little he understands the ways of the world and of God. More importantly for him, however, he at last has a direct relationship with the Lord.

Psalm 107.1–32 (or 107.1–3, 23–32): Thanksgiving is offered to the Lord who saves from storms and other dangers those who call upon God.

Second Lesson (The Epistle)   II Corinthians 5.14–21

In this lesson **Paul celebrates God's reconciling work through Christ's love and sacrificial death.** The human situation and perspective have been dramatically transformed. Those who are united to Christ are part of a new order of creation. For our sake he experienced the consequences of human sin in order that we might have a right relationship with God. Now we are ambassadors of this message of reconciliation.

The Gospel   Mark 4.35–41

The Gospel is **the story of Jesus' stilling of the storm.** The narrative was used in the life of the early church to stress the importance of faith in difficult times. Still more significantly, it served to emphasize the majesty of the Lord Jesus whose power could control destructive natural forces and, symbolically, the cosmic forces of evil. Audiences of that time would recognize the parallel between Jesus' sovereignty over the storm and the power of God shown when God, according to myth, conquered over the watery chaos and formed the world.

An introduction to a longer gospel passage, Mark 4.35–5.20, is found on p. 220.

PROPER SEVEN
(Sunday closest to June 22)

First Lesson   Zechariah 12.8–10, 13.1

Our Old Testament lesson is composed of brief **oracles of deliverance and repentance. Tears of compassion for one who suffers, together with God's mercy, bring about a cleansing from sin.** The Lord will protect all the people of the holy city, including the very weakest. They will weep and mourn as they look upon the one whom they have pierced. This figure may be an individual who suffered on behalf of the people. Christians perceive in his death a prefigurement of the passion of Jesus, and find in the cleansing that follows a reference to the forgiveness of sins through baptism.

Psalm 63.1–8: The individual seeks the Lord in whose presence there is sufficiency and contentment.

Second Lesson (The Epistle)   Galatians 3.23–29

In this New Testament lesson we hear that **the era of domination by the law is passed. Through faith all find themselves baptized into a unity in Christ.** Formerly we were like small children who had to be closely watched. Now, through God's justification, we are given the status of young adults coming into their maturity. Whatever the former barriers of race, class or sex, we are together heirs of the promise to Abraham.

The Gospel   Luke 9.18–24

In our Gospel **Peter recognizes that Jesus is the Christ, but Jesus then tells his followers of the suffering and death he must endure as the Son of Man.** The passage helps us to realize that during Jesus' lifetime and afterward there was speculation about his role. Some saw him as a kind of reembodiment of John the Baptist or of an earlier prophet. Jesus emphasizes the essential character of his ministry and teaches that his disciples must follow in his way.

PROPER EIGHT
(Sunday closest to June 29)

First Lesson   Isaiah 2.10–17

In our first lesson **the prophet announces that the day of the Lord will be a time of judgment against all that is proud and lofty.** Popular thought suggested that the day of the Lord's coming would mean defeat for Israel's enemies and victory for Israel. Instead we learn here, and in the preceding passage, that God will begin by condemning the hoarded wealth and the idolatry of God's own people. It will be a time to hide from God's wrath. In the repeated refrain, "the Lord alone will be exalted."

Psalm 89.1–18 (or 89.1–4, 15–18): The Lord is praised for faithful love and mighty justice.

Second Lesson (The Epistle)   Romans 6.3–11

In this reading we learn that, **as Christian disciples have been joined with Christ in his death through baptism, so they are to know a resurrection like his.** In union with Christ we have died to our sinful selves and have begun to experience a new way of life. In one sense, Paul recognizes, our freedom from death still awaits us in the future. Yet, in another sense, we already know what it means to be alive to God in Jesus Christ and to realize the true meaning of life.

The Gospel   Matthew 10.34–42

In the Gospel **Jesus further describes what it means to be his disciple: it is not a way of easy peace.** Deciding for or against the cost of discipleship will cause divisions even within families. But discipleship must come ahead of family—indeed, ahead of all else one counts dear. By letting go of one's hold on life the true meaning of life will be found. Those who receive Jesus' followers will find they are receiving the Lord himself and God who sent him. Those who do well and help even the least of the disciples will find reward.

PROPER EIGHT
(Sunday closest to June 29)

First Lesson   Deuteronomy 15.7–11

Our opening reading reminds of **the responsibility to be open of heart and hand toward the poor and needy.** This exhortation is preceded by teaching about the seventh or sabbatical year at the end of which all debts were to be cancelled. The practical effects of this obligation were such as to cause people to be unwilling to make any loans as the seventh year approached. The spirit of this passage asks for an attitude which goes beyond legalities.

Psalm 112: Blessed are those who are right with the Lord, who are just and generous to those in need.

Second Lesson (The Epistle)   II Corinthians 8.1–9, 13–15

In this lesson **Paul sets before the Corinthians the example of the generosity of the churches in Macedonia, and urges them to join with the same spirit into the collection being taken up for the poor Christians in Jerusalem.** Paul has two purposes in collecting this relief money. First, there is serious need in the Jerusalem community, due probably to both persecution and famine. Secondly, the apostle hopes by this means to draw the Jerusalem church and the new congregations into a profound relationship of mutual care and equality. In all this, the chief example is the Lord Jesus who in his coming to earth became poor on behalf of all.

The Gospel   Mark 5.22–24, 35b–43

The Gospel is **the story of the healing of the daughter of Jairus, an official of the local synagogue.** Even in the face of the news that the little girl is dead, Jesus persists in urging the father to have faith. The Lord's comment that the girl is not dead but sleeping tests our understanding as to whether death is the final reality. The child is past all human help, but Jesus' raising of her points beyond this narrative to the hope that will not be fully realized until his own resurrection.

PROPER EIGHT
(Sunday closest to June 29)

First Lesson   I Kings 19.15–16, 19–21

Our Old Testament reading is **the story of the calling of Elisha by Elijah to be his successor as the Lord's prophet.** Elijah is commissioned to anoint the kings of Syria and Israel and, more importantly, to anoint Elisha to a prophetic ministry. He throws his hairy prophet's cloak on Elisha who immediately recognizes what Elijah has done. Elijah leaves the decision whether or not to follow him to Elisha, who then bids his parents farewell and makes a feast of his plowing oxen.

Psalm 16 (or 16.5–11): Contentment, refuge and joy are found in the presence of the Lord.

Second Lesson (The Epistle)   Galatians 5.1, 13–25

In this lesson **Paul describes the character of Christian freedom.** It enables one to fulfill the spirit of the entire law by loving one's neighbor as oneself. But always there is the danger of lapsing back into the old ways, described here as the ways of the flesh. This means enslavement to physical and spiritual sins which result from an unwillingness to be servants to one another in love. Those who belong to Christ live by the Spirit of love, joy and self-control.

The Gospel   Luke 9.51–62

In our Gospel we hear how **Jesus on his way to Jerusalem encounters opposition and misunderstanding, and then speaks with several would-be disciples.** The Samaritans reject Jesus because they were opposed to worship in Jerusalem. James and John wish to punish them, but this is not Jesus' way. Potential followers are bid to count the cost, and Jesus points out that true discipleship means leaving other things behind. This can cause the painful rupture of past ties and relationships.

PROPER NINE
(Sunday closest to July 6)

First Lesson   Zechariah 9.9–12

Our opening reading is **a prophecy of great hope and salvation for Jerusalem: her triumphant but humble king comes to rule.** This vision of the victorious yet lowly messiah riding on a young ass derives from ancient rituals in the holy city. Several hundred years before Jesus' time the prophet Zechariah looked forward to a time of restoration for his people and a magnificent new king. His peaceful dominion will reach from the great river (the Euphrates, but mythically the river of paradise) to the ends of the earth.

Psalm 145 (or 145.8–14): A hymn of praise to the Lord, mighty in divine deeds, yet tender and compassionate.

Second Lesson (The Epistle)   Romans 7.21–8.6

In this lesson **Paul feels himself a divided man, locked in a deadly battle with the law, until set free by the Spirit through Jesus' sacrifice.** Here Paul thinks of himself almost as two persons; an inner, more spiritual and rational individual, whose higher nature wishes to obey the rightful dictates of the law, is struggling with a baser nature enslaved to sin. While this lower nature is described in terms of body and flesh, it includes all human tendencies to turn away from good. From this misery God has rescued Paul by sending Jesus, the Son of God, to take the condemnation of sin upon himself, breaking its power and making it possible now to fulfil the good purpose which lies behind the law.

The Gospel   Matthew 11.25–30

In the Gospel passage **Jesus offers thanks to the Father in heaven for the revelation God has given, and bids all to come and find that the yoke of his teaching is easy to bear.** The disclosure of the divine will comes as God's gracious gift, not through human knowledge. Especially intimate is the relationship between the Lord of all the world and Jesus—that of Father and Son. Yet, though he is the Son, he is humble of heart and gentle.

PROPER NINE
(Sunday closest to July 6)

First Lesson   Ezekiel 2.1–7

In our Old Testament lesson **Ezekiel receives his prophetic commission: he is to speak the words of the Lord fearlessly to the rebellious people of Israel.** Throughout this book God addresses Ezekiel as *son of man*, meaning human being. But while only a mortal, the Lord's Spirit is with him so that the people will know that a prophet is in their midst. He will pronounce stern judgment on a nation that has sinned and is being sent into exile.

Psalm 123: Those who are lowly and scorned place their trust in the merciful Lord.

Second Lesson (The Epistle)   II Corinthians 12.2–10

In this reading **Paul tells of both exaltation and infirmity, and the discovery of a strength that comes through weakness.** The Corinthians wanted to boast of their revelations and visions. Well, Paul knows a person (he means himself) who once had an ecstatic experience. God has, however, revealed something still more important to him: that the divine power comes to its full strength when acting through human frailty.

The Gospel   Mark 6.1–6

In our Gospel story **Jesus returns to his home town and finds suspicion and lack of faith.** He can do no mighty works in such a climate. The passage reminds us that God's action is often clothed in the commonplace. This truth humans have a hard time recognizing. It at least helps us to understand what was also a mystery and a problem for the early church: how Jesus could have been rejected by many of his own people.

PROPER NINE
(Sunday closest to July 6)

First Lesson   Isaiah 66.10–16

The first reading tells of **a time of consolation and triumphant vindication for God's people.** As the passage opens Jerusalem becomes like a comforting mother for whom the Lord provides a river of prosperity. The mixture of images continues as God also assumes the mothering role. Finally, the Lord is like a fire and is a mighty warrior against God's enemies.

Psalm 66 (or 66.1–8): A hymn of praise and thanksgiving to God who rules in majesty and delivers God's people.

Second Lesson (The Epistle)   Galatians 6.14–18

In this lesson **Paul closes his letter to the Galatians by reminding them that nothing counts in comparison with the glory of Christ's saving cross.** They are not to make the mistake of thinking that salvation is helped or hindered either by circumcision according to the law or because they are uncircumcised Gentiles. The power of the cross has formed something new, an Israel to which both Jews and Gentiles belong. Paul's own experiences as an apostle have allowed him to share in the compassion of the cross and have left him with signs of a suffering like those of Jesus.

The Gospel   Luke 10.1–12, 16–20

In the Gospel story **Jesus appoints seventy missionaries to go before him and gives them their instructions.** The number recalls the leaders who were once chosen to assist Moses in his work and signifies all the nations of the world. The narrative is meant to prefigure the evangelization of every land. The ministry of proclamation and of healing is a matter of urgency and brings judgment on all who fail to receive its messengers. The disciples are representatives of Jesus in a battle with the powers of evil.

Some early versions and modern translations read seventy-two instead of seventy. The significance of the number is the same. For the introduction to a longer second lesson, Galatians 6.1–18, see p. 220.

PROPER TEN
(Sunday closest to July 13)

First Lesson   Isaiah 55.1–5, 10–13

In our Old Testament reading we hear how **the return from exile will be a time of prosperity and abundance when God's covenant will be renewed.** The prophet pictures the great day: for a people who have been near death there will be food and drink without cost. God's covenant with David is to be extended to all Israel, and other nations will come to see her glory. The life-giving word of the Lord will not fail to produce its fruit and, together with Israel, the natural world will rejoice and reflect God's power.

Psalm 65 (or 65.9–14): A psalm of praise and thanksgiving to the savior, the mighty Lord, who creates the earth and causes it to bring forth abundantly.

Second Lesson (The Epistle)   Romans 8.9–17

In this lesson we hear that, **if we follow our lower nature, we are enslaved and destined to death, but, when moved by God's Spirit, we become God's children and heirs with Christ.** The Spirit makes the experience possible by prompting our lips to call upon God as Father with the same Aramaic word (Abba) that Jesus used. This new relationship means that we are no longer required to be led by baser instincts. Our heritage is life. Even in our mortal bodies we can begin to realize the hope of the resurrection, while we must also learn to share Christ's sufferings.

The Gospel   Matthew 13.1–9, 18–23

Our Gospel is **Jesus' parable of the sower, together with its interpretation.** The story by itself may once have been used to stress how surprisingly fruitful God's power can be, quite apart from human expectations or control. With its explanation the parable was used as an allegory by early Christians to help them understand the missionary situation of the church. Because of the work of the devil and human weakness and sin, the word they preached did not always produce. But, in the right circumstances, its fruit could be anywhere from substantial to amazing.

PROPER TEN
(Sunday closest to July 13)

First Lesson   Amos 7.7–15

In the first lesson **Amos is given a vision of a plumb line, and he prophecies God's judgment regardless of the personal consequences.** A plumb line hangs down and shows whether a wall is vertical. Israel's heart is out of line, and God is out of patience. The priest of the royal shrine at Bethel reports Amos' words to the king and tells him to prophesy elsewhere. Amos replies that he is not one of the official, professional prophets that do others' bidding; God has called him.

Psalm 85 (85.7–13): The psalm both celebrates and prays for the Lord's gracious favor, God's forgiveness, deliverance and justice.

Second Lesson (The Epistle)   Ephesians 1.1–14

In this reading **Paul greets the Christians in Ephesus and praises God for the glorious inheritance which has been ordained for those who are God's children.** Redeemed by the sacrifice of Christ, our freedom from sin is made possible. Now we share in the mystery of God's plan to form a universal community in association with Christ. In all this we have the Holy Spirit as a kind of pledge or down-payment for the fullness of the heritage to come.

The Gospel   Mark 6.7–13

In the Gospel **Jesus sends his chosen disciples out on their missionary work and gives them their instructions.** The commissioning actions of Christ are the foundation and the prefiguring of the church's essential tasks of evangelization and healing. His followers are given authority over the demonic forces of evil and are to call for repentance—a change of heart and a new way of life. Traveling in pairs, these apostles are to take practically nothing with them. Their poverty is probably intended as a sign of their authenticity and trust in God and may also indicate the urgency with which this work is to be done.

141

PROPER TEN
(Sunday closest to July 13)

First Lesson   Deuteronomy 30.9–14

The Old Testament reading offers **a promise of prosperity to the people who obey God's commandments.** This counsel is presented as the teaching of Moses. It was probably written at a later time when the law was not well observed. Yet the Lord's word is not distant or hard to understand. God has not left the divine will in doubt. It is near to hand in the commandments God has given.

Psalm 25 (or 25.3–9): A prayer for forgiveness and guidance and an expression of trust in the Lord.

Second Lesson (The Epistle)   Colossians 1.1–14

In this lesson **Paul greets the Christians at Colossae, offers thanks for their faith, and prays for their further strengthening.** Paul had apparently not visited this city in the country known today as Turkey, but he praises his fellow servant Epaphras who brought the gospel to the new converts. The apostle asks that they may be filled with spiritual understanding and be fruitful in good works. So will they give thanks to the God who has rescued them from the power of darkness and evil and brought them into the kingdom of the Son of God.

The Gospel   Luke 10.25–37

The Gospel is **the lawyer's question and the parable of the Good Samaritan.** While testing Jesus, this expert in the law asks a question at the heart of human longing: how can life's true meaning and purpose be realized? Jesus causes him to answer for himself with the summary of the law. Recognizing how hard it is to put such lofty commandments into practice, the lawyer next asks, who is the neighbor that I am to love? Jesus hears his real question (who is *not* my neighbor?) and tells him the story of a man who could help another without requiring the law's definition.

142

PROPER ELEVEN
(Sunday closest to July 20)

First Lesson   Wisdom 12.13, 16–19

In the first lesson we hear that **God, who is sovereign over all things, is also a God of mercy and forbearance.** This is the only God, and to those who disbelieve the divine power God will make it known. But chiefly God reveals power and strength in care for all and by making room for repentence. God sets an example for the people, showing how the just must be kind. (This passage comes from one of the Jewish writings composed about a century before the time of Christ but not contained in the Old Testament.)

Psalm 86 (or 86.11–17): A prayer to the gracious and loving Lord for mercy and guidance.

Second Lesson (The Epistle)   Romans 8.18–25

In this New Testament reading **Paul contrasts present suffering with the hope of the glory that is yet to be revealed.** The apostle understands the whole of creation to be linked with human destiny. As it shares in the penalty of slavery to mortality and corruption, it will, through our freedom as children of God, participate in our full redemption. This is our saving hope, still unseen, but for which we now have the first fruits of the Spirit.

The Gospel   Matthew 13.24–30, 36–43

The Gospel is **the parable of the wheat and the weeds, for which Jesus then provides an explanation.** The story points to a mystery: why there is both good and evil in life. The parable may at one time have been used to suggest that it is not so easy for humans to know what is good and what is bad from the divine perspective. In a strangely mixed world one must carry on with patience. The allegorical explanation emphasizes the judgment which will take place in the end at the hands of the Son of Man.

143

PROPER ELEVEN
(Sunday closest to July 20)

First Lesson   Isaiah 57.14b–21

In the Old Testament reading **the prophet announces that the time of punishment and the Lord's anger is ended. God heals the lowly and broken in spirit.** In one sense God is distant from human life, high and exalted. Yet God also is close to the humble. After exile and further tribulation, God offers peace and new courage. The restless wicked, however, will not know the Lord's peace.

Psalm 22.22–30: A song of praise to the Lord who rules over all and cares for the downtrodden.

Second Lesson (The Epistle)   Ephesians 2.11–22

This passage is **a celebration of the new community of a unified humanity which God has formed and built up through Christ Jesus.** Before this time Gentiles lived a life distant from God and the hope of God's promises. Now through the sacrifice of Christ the power of the law to separate and the wall of hostility are broken down. Former strangers have found peace and become fellow citizens who share in the Lord's spiritual temple.

The Gospel   Mark 6.30–44

Our Gospel lesson is **the story of Jesus' feeding of the five thousand.** The apostles return from their missionary work, but their time of rest is disturbed by a great crowd whom Jesus teaches and then feeds with the loaves and fishes. The narrative has many levels of meaning. It recalls Old Testament stories, especially God's shepherding and feeding of the Israelites with manna in the desert, and points forward to the legendary banquet at the end of time where Christ will preside. The abundant miracle illustrates Jesus' lordship; he is intimate with the power of creation. Other themes associated with the Eucharist are also present.

PROPER ELEVEN
(Sunday closest to July 20)

First Lesson   Genesis 18.1–10a

In our Old Testament story **the Lord appears to Abraham and promises that he and Sarah will have a son.** As often in these narratives the Lord's presence is disguised, this time in one of the three visitors. Abraham may suspect God's nearness, but he also generously fulfills his duty of hospitality to strangers. Despite the fact that both he and Sarah are well beyond the years of child-bearing, Abraham will place his trust in God's power and through this son become the father of a great people.

Psalm 15: The psalm describes the virtues of one who is worthy to worship the Lord.

Second Lesson (The Epistle)   Colossians 1.21–29

This lesson tells of **the revealed mystery of God's plan: that Gentiles, too, should share in the hope of glory.** For this ministry to non-Jews Paul has been especially appointed. The sufferings he experiences in his work are a way of filling out the redemptive activity of Christ through his body of the church. The result is that those who once were strangers to God and living in sin may now be reconciled through Christ's sacrifice and grow toward their maturity in his body.

The Gospel   Luke 10.38–42

The Gospel is **the story of Martha and Mary and their different attitudes toward life and the Lord's presence.** Jesus is on his way to Jerusalem and his death. The little narrative focuses on Martha and indicates how good works without a response to the Lord may only lead to anxiety and missing what is essential.

The first lesson may be lengthened so as to include all of Genesis 18.1–14. For its introduction see p. 220.

PROPER TWELVE
(Sunday closest to July 27)

First Lesson   I Kings 3.5–12

In our opening lesson **King Solomon pleases the Lord by requesting an understanding mind with which to govern the people.** God
appears to Solomon in a dream shortly after he has come to the
throne of his father David. Solomon not only wishes the skill to rule
but the wisdom to do it justly, distinguishing between good and
evil. God grants him this and much more, and Solomon will become
famous both for his wisdom and the splendor of his kingdom.

Psalm 119.121–136 (or 129–136): The psalmist continues to praise
   God's commandments and asks for guidance and the Lord's
   justice.

Second Lesson (The Epistle)   Romans 8.26–34

In this reading **Paul expresses his great confidence that God is
for us, making God's love known through the sacrifice of the Son
and the help of the Spirit.** The Spirit pleads with God for us, providing what we cannot find the words to say. We learn that God
works for good with those who love God and are called according to
divine purpose. God has set us apart to become like the Son, Jesus,
and so has made us acceptable with God. Who then can bring a
charge against us?

The Gospel   Matthew 13.31–33, 44–49a

Our Gospel is comprised of **five of Jesus' short parables: the mustard seed, the leaven, the hidden treasure, the priceless pearl, and
the net.** They suggest how the action of God's reign is realized.
What seems insignificant is suddenly of great importance. It is like a
marvelous gift which one seizes upon joyfully and for which all else
is willingly sacrificed. The kingdom takes in all kinds. Only at the
end will there be a sorting out.

PROPER TWELVE
(Sunday closest to July 27)

First Lesson   II Kings 2.1–15

From the Old Testament we hear **the story of the taking up of the prophet Elijah into heaven and the passing on of his power to Elisha.** The narrative illustrates the great favor Elijah found in the eyes of the Lord as he is carried away in a chariot of fire. Elisha is in despair, but God does not leave the people without prophetic vision. As Elijah had done before him, and like a new Joshua, Elisha proves that God is with him by causing the Jordan River to part.

Psalm 114: A song of praise to the Lord who has brought God's people from Egypt, through the wilderness and across the Jordan to the promised land.

Second Lesson (The Epistle)   Ephesians 4.1–7, 11–16

In this lesson **the new Christians in Ephesus are urged to lead lives of patient love, using their various gifts in the unity of the Spirit, while growing toward their maturity in Christ.** There are many roles of service, but there is a oneness at the heart of the faith and in its goal. All the disciples' efforts are meant to build up the one body of Christ. While there remains a human perversity leading toward division, in the loving truth of the community Christians are to grow together toward their full humanity.

The Gospel   Mark 6.45–52

The Gospel is **the story of Jesus' walking on the water.** The narrative has been given a variety of interpretations. In legendary terms Jesus is like the Creator God who triumphs over the watery chaos monster. Mark, the evangelist, stresses the disciples' inability fully to understand Jesus' purpose in this act or in the feeding of the five thousand. Later a church under persecution would perceive in the story the saving presence of their risen Lord.

PROPER TWELVE
(Sunday closest to July 27)

First Lesson   Genesis 18.20–33

In our first reading **the patriarch Abraham bargains with the Lord over the fate of Sodom. He learns how ready the Lord is to turn away divine anger for the sake of the few who are good.** Abraham dares just a little further each time in testing the Lord's patience. In this period the presence of a few wicked persons was thought to make an entire community liable to judgment. This story, which applies the principle in reverse, represents a significant advance in Israel's understanding of God: mercy directs God's actions.

Psalm 138: A hymn of praise and thanksgiving to the Lord on high, who has saved God's servant and cares for the lowly.

Second Lesson (The Epistle)   Colossians 2.6–15

In this lesson **the new disciples at Colossae are urged to remain rooted in Christ, letting nothing detract from his uniqueness and preeminence.** The Colossians were apparently tempted to worship the pagan star-gods along with Jesus, and also to accept basic Jewish practices such as circumcision as necessary to salvation. But God has revealed the fullness of divinity in Christ, who has triumphed over all such gods. The record of our sin and debt to law have been nailed to the cross. Ours is a far better spiritual circumcision found through dying to our sinful self and being made alive with Christ.

The Gospel   Luke 11.1–13

In the Gospel lesson **Jesus teaches his disciples about prayer and the character of God as Father.** This shorter version of the Lord's Prayer is the earliest known to us. Its concern is both with present life and with readiness for the coming of the reign of God. Jesus' two little stories encourage his followers continually to ask in prayer and to expect the good gifts of God, especially the Holy Spirit.

PROPER THIRTEEN
(Sunday closest to August 3)

First Lesson   Nehemiah 9.16–20

In our Old Testament lesson **the scribe Ezra recalls how patient and gracious the Lord was when leading the people through the wilderness on the way to the promised land.** Ezra is remembering these events at a much later time, in a restored Jerusalem when the traditions are being reestablished and understood. Ezra thanks God for protecting and feeding the people despite their stubbornness and idolatry. His words offer hope that God will again be gracious in spite of sins.

Psalm 78.1–29 (or 78.14–20, 23–25): The psalm recalls Israel's trials and the Lord's sustaining grace in the wilderness after the escape from Egypt.

Second Lesson (The Epistle)   Romans 8.35–39

In this reading **Paul exults because we can never be separated from the saving love of God in Christ.** As scripture indicates, we still have many hardships to undergo. But even in tribulation we find the conquering power of God's love which has been shown in the cross. No dangers of human life, or supernatural powers, either present or future, can come between us and this love.

The Gospel   Matthew 14.13–21

Our Gospel is **the story of Jesus' feeding of over five thousand persons.** After the death of John the Baptist Jesus seeks a time of retreat. The crowds, however, follow him, and he has compassion on them. The narrative suggests many levels of meaning. It recalls Old Testament stories, especially God's feeding of the Israelites with manna in the wilderness, and points forward to the legendary banquet at the end of time where Christ will preside. The abundant miracle illustrates Jesus' lordship; he is intimate with the powers of creation. Other themes associated with the Eucharist are also close at hand.

PROPER THIRTEEN
(Sunday closest to August 3)

First Lesson   Exodus 16.2–4, 9–15

From the Old Testament we hear **the story of God's feeding of the people in the wilderness.** The Israelites are full of complaints and now think they would prefer slavery and death in Egypt to their present difficulties. The Lord appears to them and promises sustenance, but also a test, for they will only be given food on a day-to-day basis. It is possible to explain the food in natural terms: the flock of quail provide flesh and the secretion of insects the bread-like substance. But the point of the narrative is that God provides. The Israelites call the bread manna (perhaps from words meaning "What is this?").

Psalm 78.1–25 (or 78.14–20, 23–25): The psalm recalls Israel's trials and the Lord's sustaining grace in the wilderness after the escape from Egypt.

Second Lesson (The Epistle)   Ephesians 4.17–25

In this reading **the new converts at Ephesus are reminded of their former style of life and urged to put on their new nature.** The pagan life is a way of darkness and vice. In Christ the deceitful lusts of the old nature have been put off. The new nature is according to God's likeness and image. The language of putting off and on, together with other images, is meant to recall Christian baptism. We are now members one of another in the body of Christ.

The Gospel   John 6.24–35

In our Gospel **Jesus tells the crowd of the true bread of life, the bread from heaven.** The people follow Jesus after he has fed the crowd of five thousand, but they come mostly to obtain more food for their stomachs. The bread which the Son of Man offers is more genuinely life-giving than the manna by which Israel was fed in the wilderness. In one sense this means that Jesus' teaching is greater than that of Moses. More significantly still, it is belief in Jesus himself that leads to eternal life.

PROPER THIRTEEN
(Sunday closest to August 3)

First Lesson   Ecclesiastes 1.12–14; 2.18–23

In our opening reading **the Teacher reflects on the useless character of life and the fact that the fruit of all our labors will be inherited by others.** The author (who fictionally is King Solomon) refers to himself as Qoheleth, which is variously translated as Teacher, Preacher or Philosopher. His view of existence is pessimistic. His study indicates that everything we do is a chasing after the wind and that God's ways are unknown. It is one of the Bible's remarkable features that it includes this very human attitude together with other views which suggest God's purposes for creation.

Psalm 49 (or 49.1–11): The psalmist speaks words of wisdom: wise and foolish, rich and poor alike, all will die. We cannot pay the price for our lives.

Second Lesson (The Epistle)   Colossians 3.12–17

In this New Testament lesson **disciples are urged to clothe themselves with Christian virtues and, with thankfulness in their hearts, to do everything in the name of the Lord Jesus.** These new converts are among God's chosen people. They are to forgive as God has forgiven them and to live in peace. As members of one body, they should teach one another with wisdom, while all is bound together in love.

The Gospel   Luke 12.13–21

In our Gospel **Jesus warns against greed and tells the story of an individual who was rich only in material possessions.** The Lord refuses to be the judge in a matter having to do with inheritance and wealth. Life lived without reference to God is empty and foolish. Despite all our plans and efforts at security, the fact of death makes this very clear.

The first lesson may be lengthened to Ecclesiastes 1.12–14; 2.1–7, 11, 18–23, and the second lesson to Colossians 3.5–17. Their introductions are on p. 221.

151

PROPER FOURTEEN
(Sunday closest to August 10)

First Lesson   Jonah 2.1–9

In our Old Testament story **Jonah, who tried to flee from the Lord's calling only to be cast overboard and swallowed by a great fish, now prays to the Lord from the fish's belly.** The language of his prayer recalls certain of the psalms, where suffering and tribulation are spoken of in terms of drowning and being near Sheol or death. Israel's experiences of exile and exodus could also be described with these images. Jonah promises, after he is saved, to offer sacrifices in the temple.

Psalm 29: The majesty of God is described in the likeness of a thunderstorm: the Lord is mighty over land and sea.

Second Lesson (The Epistle)   Romans 9.1–5

In this reading **Paul expresses his anguish and sorrow that so many of the children of Israel, the people especially favored by God, have not found the Lord's promise.** To them belong the covenants, the law and so much else. From their nation Christ himself came. Paul would go to great lengths, even see himself an outcast, if such would help Israel to know its salvation. Later in this letter Paul tries to explain how this all may be part of God's plan of redemption, which in the end will include Israel with the Gentiles.

The Gospel   Matthew 14.22–33

The Gospel is the story of **Jesus' walking on the water and his rescue of Peter after his faith fails him.** The narrative has several levels of meaning. In legendary terms Jesus is like the creator God who strides over the watery chaos monster. Matthew's Gospel stresses this revelation of Jesus' close relationship with God, as God's Son, and the importance of faith on the part of the disciples. A church beset by its own problems and lack of faith would be glad to perceive in this story the saving presence of its risen Lord.

PROPER FOURTEEN
(Sunday closest to August 10)

First Lesson   Deuteronomy 8.1–10

In our Old Testament reading **Moses reminds the people of their responsibility to keep the Lord's commandments, and of God's testing of them and gracious protection during their long journey through the wilderness to the promised land.** Continually Israel did not measure up in its trials. They rebelled and had to endure hardships. All this was a matter of discipline. They were without food and then received manna from the Lord in order to learn that their most essential sustenance comes from God.

Psalm 34 (or 34.1–8): A hymn of blessing and praise to the Lord for divine deliverance.

Second Lesson (The Epistle)   Ephesians 4.30–5.2

In this lesson **Christians are urged to conform to a new way of life which is pleasing to the Holy Spirit. They are to have a love like the love of Christ.** The new converts are to show great care and generosity toward one another. They must put away all kinds of spitefulness since these harm the bond of unity and grieve the Spirit with which they have been sealed in baptism. The model is none other than God as God is revealed in the Christ who sacrificed himself for us.

The Gospel   John 6.37–51

In our Gospel **Jesus continues to teach that he is the true bread who will bring all who have faith in him to eternal life.** The discussion is meant to recall the story of the Israelites protesting and murmuring against God in the wilderness because they had no bread. But even the manna that God gave them was only a temporary food. While Jesus seems very ordinary to many of the people of his time, he offers the world both his teaching and himself, a life-giving bread from heaven.

The second lesson may be lengthened to Ephesians 4.25–5.2. For an introduction to this longer reading see p. 221.

153

PROPER FOURTEEN
(Sunday closest to August 10)

First Lesson   Genesis 15.1–6

In our first reading **the Lord visits Abraham and promises that he will have a son and descendants in number like the stars.** Because he had no son Abraham (whose name at one time was Abram) had chosen one of his slaves to be his heir. But now he believes the Lord, and through his son Isaac becomes the father of Israel. Christians will later understand Abraham to be the father of all who put their trust in the Lord and find that God has accepted them into a right relationship.

Psalm 33 (or 33.12–15, 18–22): Joyful are the people who trust in the Lord. From heaven God sees all who dwell on the earth.

Second Lesson (The Epistle)   Hebrews 11.1–3, 8–16

In this New Testament lesson **faith is described as a holding fast to things hoped for and learning to trust in their reality. Abraham is among those who had such a faith.** Noah is another of the great figures of the Old Testament who found a right relationship with God through faith. But Abraham, who trusted God's word that he would have many descendants, is our chief example. As he left his own country for the promised land, so we now look forward in faith to the promise of a heavenly country.

The Gospel   Luke 12.32–40

In the Gospel **Jesus teaches his disciples to trust entirely in the reign of God, their Father, and to be ever ready for the coming of the Son of Man.** The kingdom is God's gift. Disciples are to respond by letting go their hold on worldly possessions and giving their heart to a treasure that is heavenly. They are to remember the householder who would have kept his house safe if he knew when the thief was coming. They are to be like servants alert for the return of their master whenever he comes. Like the Lord of the Eucharist, he will then wait on them.

The second lesson may be lengthened to include Hebrews 11.4–7. In an introduction to this reading the third sentence above should begin: "Abel, Enoch and Noah are other great figures . . ."

PROPER FIFTEEN
(Sunday closest to August 17)

First Lesson   Isaiah 56.1, 6–7

In our opening lesson **the Lord exhorts the people to do what is just because the time of his righteous salvation is close at hand. The temple will be a house of prayer for all nations.** This vision of hope emphasizes the outgoing aspects of Israel's faith. Historically it deals with the fact that after the exile certain non-Israelites had come to live in Jerusalem and serve in the temple. The passage sets the conditions for their participation, but also looks beyond to a day when many peoples will worship the God of Israel.

Psalm 67: A prayer for God's graciousness and saving power, and a bidding of praise by all people for God's justice and bounty.

Second Lesson (The Epistle)   Romans 11.13–15, 29–32

In this reading **Paul sets forth his belief that God plans to bring Jews as well as Gentiles to salvation.** The apostle to the Gentiles continues to wrestle with a difficult question: why so many of Jesus' own people have not accepted him as the Christ. In the first place, it was their unbelief that helped make it possible for the gospel with its Jewish heritage to be taken to many new people. It also made the Jews equal with Gentiles in that all had now been disobedient to God. In the next step the Jewish people will see the mercy shown to the Gentiles and want themselves to share in it in their own way.

The Gospel   Matthew 15.21–28

The Gospel is **the story of Jesus' conversation with the Canaanite woman and his healing of her daughter.** The narrative was especially important to the early church because it showed Jesus' power reaching out beyond the borders of Judaism. The first Christians were unsure whether they were to offer the faith to non-Jews, and the give and take in the story reflects the uncertainty. Jesus sees his own mission as confined to Israel, but the woman's faith causes him to give her the bread she asks for. Symbolically it is the saving food of the gospel which heals her daughter.

The first lesson may be lengthened to Isaiah 56.1–7. See p. 222.

PROPER FIFTEEN
(Sunday closest to August 17)

First Lesson   Proverbs 9.1–6

In our opening lesson **Wisdom is pictured as a gracious hostess who invites the ignorant and foolish to her table.** Several centuries before the time of Christ, *Wisdom* was understood to be an important characteristic of God and was often described as a judicious woman who spoke to human hearts and minds. In this way some of the feeling of distance between the people and the transcendent God was overcome. Those who heed Wisdom's counsels and do not follow the seduction of folly will be blessed.

Psalm 147: A hymn of praise to the Lord who rules over nature in wisdom and has shown faithfulness to God's people Israel.

Second Lesson (The Epistle)   Ephesians 5.15–20

In this reading **the new Christians in Ephesus are bid to live wisely and, glad with songs, to give thanks for everything to God.** Instead of following drunken ways, symbolic of all kinds of foolish behavior, they are to be filled with the Holy Spirit. Because the time is in the grip of evil, opportunities to do the will of the Lord must be used to the full.

The Gospel   John 6.53–59

In the Gospel lesson **Jesus speaks of the flesh and blood of the Son of Man as the bread from heaven which must be eaten in order to share in the life of the eternal age.** Previously in this Gospel the bread of life had seemed to signify Jesus' teaching and his presence. Now it is given still more significance with the understanding that the believer may share deeply in the life of Jesus and his self-offering. This experience is enacted in the Holy Communion.

PROPER FIFTEEN
(Sunday closest to August 17)

First Lesson   Jeremiah 23.23–29

In our first reading **God speaks through the prophet: this is a God lofty and distant as well as near, and God knows the lies of the false prophets.** In Jeremiah's time there were many individuals who appointed themselves prophets. They said the Lord was close to them, and they relied on dreams for their inspiration. They told people the comfortable things they wanted to hear and led them into false worship. But the words of the Lord are words of judgment to the people, like scorching fire or a hammer on rock.

Psalm 82: God pronounces judgment on the heavenly beings who have failed to defend the weak and the poor. The people call on the one true God to judge and rule the earth.

Second Lesson (The Epistle)   Hebrews 12.1–7, 11–14

In this lesson **suffering and persecution are interpreted as forms of God's discipline to prepare the children of God for their destiny of holiness.** They should be taken as signs of affection, for a father only troubles himself to discipline those true children whom he loves. Such training is unpleasant at the time, but it toughens us for life's race. In all this we have not only the witnesses to faith of the Old Testament, but above all Jesus, the forerunner of our faith, who endured the cross before entering into joy.

The Gospel   Luke 12.49–56

In our Gospel passage **Jesus foresees difficult times ahead: his own ordeal and the necessity of division even within families.** He has come to bring the purifying fire of judgment, and must himself first undergo the baptism of suffering and death. Before there is any peace on earth, hard decisions leading to ruptures have to be made. The people should be like good weather-watchers in reading the signs of the times.

The second lesson may be expanded to include all of Hebrews 12. 1–14. The introduction above is also suitable for the longer reading.

PROPER SIXTEEN
(Sunday closest to August 24)

First Lesson   Isaiah 51.1–6

In our opening reading **the Lord promises those who seek God's justice that salvation will come quickly.** This is the same God who made good the divine promise to Abraham and Sarah. Now the devastation of the exile is ending. There will be joy in Zion, and the victory of God's judgment over all the earth. The heavens and earth will waste away, but God's deliverance is forever.

Psalm 138: A hymn of praise and thanksgiving to the Lord on high who has saved God's servant and cares for the lowly.

Second Lesson (The Epistle)   Romans 11.33–36

In this lesson **Paul praises God for wisdom and ways beyond human knowing.** The apostle has been trying to explain God's purposes in Israel's rejection of Jesus, while maintaining his faith that this people will also be brought to their salvation. Yet in the last analysis one can only rely on the riches of the Lord's unsearchable judgments, for on God all creation depends.

The Gospel   Matthew 16.13–20

In our Gospel **Peter realizes that Jesus is the Christ, and Jesus then sees Peter as the rock foundation for his church and gives to him the keys of the kingdom.** The passage helps us to recognize that during Jesus' lifetime and afterward there was speculation about his role. Some saw the Son of Man as a kind of reembodiment of John the Baptist or another prophet. Simon is renamed Peter (which means rock) for on him and because of this revelation the church will be built, although Jesus' messiahship must be kept secret for the present. To Peter are given the keys to open or shut the gates of the kingdom and so to make judgment.

PROPER SIXTEEN
(Sunday closest to August 24)

First Lesson   Joshua 24.1–2a, 14–24

In the Old Testment lesson **Joshua calls the people to renew their covenant with the Lord and to realize what it means to promise to worship the Lord as the only God.** This takes place at Shechem after the journey through the wilderness to the promised land. Joshua's farewell speech is stern, for it is no easy matter to enter into relationship with such a holy Lord who will not allow followers to reverence any other gods. (Historically it is possible that this ceremony was used to accept into the covenant peoples living in Palestine who were not themselves participants in the exodus.)

Psalm 16: Contentment, refuge and joy are found in the presence of the Lord. Those who follow other gods will know trouble without end. **Or** Psalm 34.15–22: The Lord is gracious toward all who turn from evil and have reverence for God.

Second Lesson (The Epistle)   Ephesians 5.21–33

In this reading **the new Christians in Ephesus are urged to show a mutual submissiveness to one another out of reverence to Christ—wives being subject to their husbands and husbands loving their wives.** With reference to the Genesis story, marriage is seen as a divine institution and is given a meaning symbolic of the intimate relationship between Christ and his church. In one sense this teaching about marriage remains within the limits of its time and social setting. Yet, at heart, there is present a vision of reciprocal love and yielding which leads to a new understanding of married life.

The Gospel   John 6.60–69

In the Gospel we hear of **different responses to Jesus' claim that he is the heavenly bread which gives the life of the eternal age to those who eat it.** His are words of spirit and life, but many can understand them only in a materialistic sense and are like the Israelites who did not trust God in the wilderness. Yet, if this saying is hard for them to believe, more difficult still will be Jesus' ascent into heaven as the Son of Man. As Jesus knew would happen, many disciples now turn away, but Peter confesses him to be God's holy one who has the words of eternal life.

159

PROPER SIXTEEN
(Sunday closest to August 24)

First Lesson   Isaiah 28.14–22

In our opening lesson **the prophet denounces the rulers of the people for making a protective covenant with the powers of the underworld and death.** Isaiah is probably referring to political alliances made with foreign nations. These deceitful intrigues will not help in the scourge to come. Instead the Lord has set in Zion the cornerstone of the divine promise to David for a lasting kingship. Using justice for a measuring line and honesty for a plumb-line, God will sweep away all lies and false security.

Psalm 46: The earth may be moved and kingdoms shaken, but God is our refuge.

Second Lesson (The Epistle)   Hebrews 12.18–19, 22–29

In this reading **disciples are said to stand, not before Mount Sinai, but before Mount Zion of the heavenly Jerusalem. Theirs is an unshakable kingdom.** The covenant at Sinai was made in terror. Through the covenant brought about by Jesus' sacrifice, the new people become God's children. Not to heed the voice of Christ, however, is more dangerous than it was not to hear God's words spoken through Moses. The God of fire who shook the earth at Sinai will shake earth and heaven once more. Only what is unshaken will remain.

The Gospel   Luke 13.22–30

In our Gospel **Jesus teaches of the narrow door to salvation. Mere association with him will not be enough to assure a place in the kingdom.** The little story of the householder who has locked his door also suggests that the opportunity of the reign of God is not available indefinitely. Now is the time for decision. Yet, while many who might expect a seat in the kingdom will be rejected, others will come from the four corners of the earth to sit at the banquet.

PROPER SEVENTEEN
(Sunday closest to August 31)

First Lesson   Jeremiah 15.15–21

In the first reading **Jeremiah complains to the Lord about the pain and difficulties of his mission. He then receives God's answer.** The prophet has been called to preach a message of dark judgment to a people who are soon to be sent into exile. Despite persecution, the Lord's words were at first a joy to Jeremiah, but God has become like a treacherous brook—a stream that dried up when its waters were needed. Then the Lord tells Jeremiah that it is he who needs to turn again to God. The Lord will be with him, and he will be a wall of bronze against the people.

Psalm 26 (or 26.1–8): A plea for justice by one who serves the Lord well.

Second Lesson (The Epistle)   Romans 12.1–8

In this lesson **Paul urges the Christians in Rome to devote themselves to God's service and to recognize that, with different functions, they are all members of one body.** Instead of dead animals, they are to offer themselves as living sacrifices. Their way of life is to be quite different from worldly standards. So will they know the will of God. All are to live in humility, realizing that they have their various gifts through God's grace.

The Gospel   Matthew 16.21–27

In the Gospel reading **Jesus teaches Peter and the other disciples that the way of his ministry and theirs is the way of the cross.** Peter had just confessed Jesus to be the Christ, but now he cannot accept the idea of the Christ being put to death. Jesus calls Peter Satan because his words represent a temptation to him. Jesus' way costs no less than everything and leads to the discovery of that which is priceless. In the end the Son of Man will come as judge to repay all people for what they have done.

161

PROPER SEVENTEEN
(Sunday closest to August 31)

First Lesson   Deuteronomy 4.1–9

In our first reading **Moses urges the people to keep the Lord's commandments in order that they and their children may live well in the promised land.** The long journey through the wilderness is nearly over, and here Moses is presented speaking to the people shortly before his death. They are to remember what happened to those of their company who worshiped the god or Baal of Peor. Instead they are to observe the Lord's statutes and so become known as a great and wise people with a just law and a God close at hand.

Psalm 15: The psalm describes the virtures of one who is worthy to worship the Lord.

Second Lesson (The Epistle)   Ephesians 6.10–20

In the New Testament lesson **Christians are instructed to put on the whole armor of God in order to defend themselves from the powers of evil which are beyond any human control.** The passage recognizes that it is God who will take the active role against these superhuman forces. In this battle it is the Christian's primary task to stand and resist. The language and imagery may once have been used in an address to newly baptized disciples. Finally they are urged to be constant in prayer, remembering Paul who is now in prison.

The Gospel   Mark 7.1–8, 14–15, 21–23

In the Gospel passage **Jesus denounces those who find ways to ignore the genuine commandments of God, and he calls people to the awareness that the only evil which can corrupt a person comes from within.** His judgments are occasioned by an accusation against his disciples that they are not following the rules of ritual cleansing. On one level Jesus' words warn against the human tendency to fashion traditions which become more important than the law itself. More significantly still, his teaching points to the dangers involved in making legalism the basis for one's life.

PROPER SEVENTEEN
(Sunday closest to August 31)

First Lesson   Ecclesiasticus 10.12–18

Our opening lesson is **a condemnation of human pride which instructs that the Lord pulls down the mighty and puts the humble in their place.** The root of pride is in the sin of a human refusal to recognize dependence on God. Individuals, especially rulers, and nations which are arrogant will be brought to destruction. (These judgments are part of a collection of proverbs and wisdom sayings composed about two centuries before the time of Christ and included in the Apocrypha.)

Psalm 112: Blessed are those who are right with the Lord, who revere God and are just and generous to those in need.

Second Lesson (The Epistle)   Hebrews 13.1–8

In this reading **Christians are urged to live moral, hospitable and charitable lives, recalling the faith and examples of their leaders, but especially the unchanging Jesus.** The leaders referred to are the founders of this church who have now died. Jesus Christ, however, remains with his people, in the past, present and future. Scripture says that God will never forsake us, and, with the Lord as our helper, there is no need to be afraid.

The Gospel   Luke 14.1, 7–14

In the Gospel **Jesus tells a parable about humility and teaches his host that he should invite the poor and infirm to his feasts.** Both the parable and the teaching have a still deeper significance. The reign of God is the Lord's gift which comes to those who do not presume their place in it. By his actions as well as his words Jesus' ministry shows that the kingdom is open to those whom others consider outcast. People who share in God's ruling love and justice are to have a transformed attitude toward the poor and needy.

For an introduction to a longer first lesson, Ecclesiasticus 10.7–18, see p. 222.

PROPER EIGHTEEN
(Sunday closest to September 7)

First Lesson   Ezekiel 33.7–11

In our Old Testament reading **the prophet Ezekiel is like a watchman: it is his responsibility to warn the wicked, but it is the individual's responsibility to stop sinning.** Some people say it is too late to repent—that the burden of past sins is too great to overcome. Ezekiel is to tell them that it is the living God which calls them to cease sinning and find life. These oracles were delivered as Israel's exile was beginning and were meant to install both a sense of accountability and the hope necessary for repentance.

Psalm 119.33–48 (or 33–40): The psalmist asks for the Lord's guidance and promises to keep God's commandments always.

Second Lesson (The Epistle)   Romans 12.9–21

In this lesson **Paul exhorts the disciples in Rome to live lives full of Christian dedication and virtue, overcoming evil with good.** One hears strong echoes of Jesus' beatitudes. Also present is Paul's own emphasis on the central role of love together with the importance of a readiness to share in both the joy and sorrow of others. Blended with these teachings are some of the best of both Jewish and pagan ethical counsel. The apostle concludes with the insistence that revenge cannot be a motivation of Christians; final justice must be left to divine retribution.

The Gospel   Matthew 18.15–20

Our Gospel presents **teaching about how to deal with sin and grievances within the Christian community.** The early churches did not have established codes and regulations and had to fashion their own ways of dealing with such matters. Here every effort is made to bring the sinful member to repentance. Failing this, the individual is to be treated as outside the church. Such decisions are understood to be ratified in heaven and by Christ's presence even in the smallest of Christian gatherings.

The first lesson may be lengthened to Ezekiel 33.1–11. The introduction above is suitable for the longer lection.

PROPER EIGHTEEN
(Sunday closest to September 7)

First Lesson   Isaiah 35.4–7a

In the Old Testament reading **God comes in judgment to save the exiled people, and the prophet foresees a time of healing.** The blind will see; the deaf hear; the lame leap; and the dumb sing. Retribution will fall upon God's enemies, but Israel will be saved. Even in the wilderness pools of water shall spring up for them. Oracles such as this became for Judaism visions of the Lord's final salvation. Christians believe the healing age to have begun with Jesus.

Psalm 146 (or 146.4–9): A hymn of praise to the Lord, who forms the world and rules in justice, who heals and cares for the needy.

Second Lesson (The Epistle)   James 1.17–27

This lesson consists of **a series of teachings on the meaning of true religion: doing God's word.** Every good gift comes from the unchanging Father. By God's word of truth we are given birth and have a first place among all God's creatures. Purified from anger and all other bad conduct, we are not only to hear God's word but to put it into practice. So do we observe the perfect law which sets people free—the law as interpreted by Jesus.

The Gospel   Mark 7.31–37

In the Gospel **Jesus heals a man who is deaf and has an impediment in his speech.** The healing is understood as a fulfillment of Isaiah's prophecy concerning what is to take place as the new age dawns. The story is unusual in that emphasis is given to the means used by Jesus for the cure. The man may be seen as a model for the healed disciple who is now able both to hear and to proclaim the Lord's teaching. This miracle is part of a series of stories revealing who Jesus really is, although this could not be widely known at the time.

165

PROPER EIGHTEEN
(Sunday closest to September 7)

First Lesson   Deuteronomy 30.15–20

In the Old Testament lesson **Moses presents the people with their choice: love and obey the Lord and find life, or turn away to other gods and know death.** Israel is about to cross over into the promised land, and this is Moses' final charge to them. In historical terms the speech was probably composed many hundreds of years later, near the time of the exile, after Israel had experienced much backsliding from the Lord. But this is still their choice: blessing or curse—life and good, or death and evil.

Psalm 1: The Lord makes fruitful the lives of those who choose the way of righteousness.

Second Lesson (The Epistle)   Philemon 1–20

This reading contains most of **the letter which Paul sent to Philemon asking that he receive back in love the runaway slave Onesimus who was voluntarily returning to him.** Other information indicates that Philemon and Onesimus came from the community of the Colossians. Paul himself is now in prison, perhaps in Rome. Onesimus means "the useful one," and Paul describes him as a man who has now become very useful. Evidently he had recently been converted to Christ. Paul does not speak against the institution of slavery, but tells Philemon that his relationship with Onesimus is changed now that they are brothers in Christ.

The Gospel   Luke 14.25–33

In our Gospel **Jesus speaks of the necessity of counting the full cost of discipleship.** To follow Jesus in the way of the cross means to surrender the whole of one's life. Any relationship which interferes with this primary commitment must be hated. Jesus tells the crowds two stories to make them consider carefully whether they are ready and able to follow him completely.

PROPER NINETEEN
(Sunday closest to September 14)

First Lesson   Ecclesiasticus 27.30–28.7

Our opening lesson is **a counsel to let go of anger and replace it with the same forgiveness which we ask for ourselves.** Those who are vengeful will know the Lord's vengeance. Those who forgive will be forgiven. How can those who are unmerciful expect mercy from the Lord? Remembering our mortality and the commandments and covenant of God, we are to overlook the faults of others. (This advice, composed about two centuries before the time of Christ, represents some of the highest ideals of Judaism and found its place in the collection of books called the Apocrypha.)

Psalm 103 (or 103.8–13): A hymn of blessing in thanksgiving for healing forgiveness and for all the Lord's acts of compassion and justice.

Second Lesson (The Epistle)   Romans 14.5–12

In this reading **Paul calls upon the Roman disciples to live with tolerance for one another's scruples, recognizing that everything can be done to honor the Lord with whom each Christian has a relationship.** Especially should those who are strong and untroubled in their consciences respect the attitudes of the weak in matters such as observing certain days and eating meat. It is possible that there was tension in the Roman church between liberal Gentile Christians and more scrupulous Jewish Christians. God, Paul reminds them, is the one to whom final answer must be given, and the risen Christ is Lord of all.

The Gospel   Matthew 18.21–35

In the Gospel lesson **Jesus bids his disciples to offer a forgiveness which is, for all practical purposes, unlimited, and he tells a parable about a man who, although forgiven much, still himself had no mercy.** Jesus has extended to all manner of people God's amazingly generous offer of acceptance into the kingdom. Those who have been so forgiven must show mercy to others. Their own forgiveness may otherwise be revoked.

PROPER NINETEEN
(Sunday closest to September 14)

First Lesson   Isaiah 50.4–9

Our first reading tells of **the servant who speaks for the Lord and suffers persecution, but still trusts in God's help and vindication.** This is the third of the "servant songs" which come from a period late in Israel's exile. The servant might be thought to be the faithful of Israel, the prophet himself, or another historical or idealized figure. The people are weary and tired of the Lord's calling, but the servant steadfastly continues. Christians have long perceived in these words a foretelling of Jesus' mission.

Psalm 116 (or 116.1–8): An offering of thanksgiving and praise by one who has been rescued from death.

Second Lesson (The Epistle)   James 2.1–5, 8–10, 14–18

In this lesson **disciples are called upon not to show favoritism for the rich over the poor, but to put faith into living practice, loving their neighbors as themselves.** The passage echoes Jesus' words and actions: the offer of the kingdom is for all, but especially for the poor and outcast who might otherwise think themselves rejected. In all we do, the law of neighbor love is sovereign. Those in need are not helped by pious thoughts and words. Faith has meaning only when it is enacted.

The Gospel   Mark 8.27–38

In the Gospel **Peter recognizes that Jesus is the Christ, and Jesus then describes the true nature of the ministry of the Son of Man and what it means to follow in his way.** The passage reminds us that during Jesus' lifetime and afterward there was speculation about his role. Some saw him as a kind of reembodiment of John the Baptist or another prophet. Peter is called Satan because his words are a temptation to turn away from the suffering and death which come before resurrection. Disciples must also learn that the true self and true life are found by those who will let themselves be lost for the sake of Jesus and the gospel.

PROPER NINETEEN
(Sunday closest to September 14)

First Lesson   Exodus 32.1, 7–14

In our Old Testament story **the people worship an idol, but Moses' prayer saves them from the Lord's punishment.** In one way or another this pattern is repeated throughout Israel's history. The people have just made a solemn covenant with God, but quickly they lose faith and want to put their trust in some more tangible and *useful* religion. In this case the object of their worship is a bull-calf, a divinity among the Canaanites and a symbol of strength and virility. Moses intercedes against the Lord's wrath and reminds him of his past help and commitment to this people.

Psalm 51.1–18 (or 1–11): A confession of sin and guilt and a prayer for a clean heart.

Second Lesson (The Epistle)   I Timothy 1.12–17

In this lesson **Paul gives thanks to the Lord Jesus and praise to God for the salvation of sinners, among whom Paul has led the way.** The apostle (or a later author writing for him) recalls his acts of persecution and blasphemy against Jesus. But the Lord was merciful to him in his ignorance and unbelief, as he has been to all who have come in faith to him.

The Gospel   Luke 15.1–10

In the Gospel **Jesus tells the two parables of the finding of the lost sheep and the lost coin.** The setting helps us to understand that Jesus may have told the story about the lost sheep to defend his acts of reaching out to share the invitation of the reign of God with those often regarded as beyond God's concern. In several ways it would be foolish to leave many sheep to go after one stray, but the parable emphasizes the lengths to which both Jesus and God will go to bring back one who is missing. The second story illustrates a related theme of the first: the great joy which is experienced when the lost is found.

PROPER TWENTY
(Sunday closest to September 21)

First Lesson   Jonah 3.10–4.11

In our Old Testament story **the Lord teaches Jonah a lesson when the prophet is angry because God is merciful to the repentant pagan city which Jonah has gone to great trouble to denounce.** "I knew it," Jonah says, in effect, when the Lord spares Nineveh; "that's why I tried to avoid your mission in the first place, because you are such a gracious God, even toward non-Israelites." The Lord causes a shrub to grow up and provide shade for the prophet. Jonah is again angry when it dies. If Jonah would have mercy for the plant, should God not be gracious toward this whole city?

Psalm 145 (or 145.1–8): A hymn of praise to the Lord, mighty in deeds, yet tender and compassionate.

Second Lesson (The Epistle)   Philippians 1.21–27

In this reading **Paul tells the Philippians that he would prefer to be with Christ beyond death, but he recognizes that he still has good work to do in his earthly life.** The passage suggests that Paul had reason to think his death might be near, perhaps by martyrdom. He looks forward to a closer union with Christ, but believes it more likely that he will be able to visit the Philippians again. Either way, he asks that they live worthily of the gospel and stand firm in unity with one another.

The Gospel   Matthew 20.1–16

Our Gospel **is the story of the laborers in the vineyard who are all paid the same wage despite their different hours of work.** Like most parables this story can have many meanings, as have been given to it in the life of the church. On one level it suggests that nobody can presume on God's grace which God often offers to those who may seem the least deserving. The parable deliberately flies in the face of normal human expectations. It offers a clue pointing to God's extraordinary evenhandedness in dealing with people quite apart from human ideas about their merit. Jesus may have told it in defense of his own sharing in the lives of the outcast.

PROPER TWENTY
(Sunday closest to September 21)

First Lesson   Wisdom 1.16–2.1, 12–22

The first reading describes **the philosophy of deluded sinners who find no purpose in life and persecute the one who is righteous.** They not only wish to take advantage of the good man, but want also to test him and finally to put him to death because his very goodness is a reproach to their way of life. They will make trial both of the one who sees himself as God's son and the God whom he believes will protect him. Blinded by their wickedness, they perceive neither God's purposes nor God's rewards for the blameless. Christians have seen in these words a foreshadowing of Christ's sufferings and vindication.

Psalm 54: A prayer for salvation by one who is persecuted.

Second Lesson (The Epistle)   James 3.16–4.6

In this New Testament lesson **the wisdom which brings peace is contrasted with jealousy, ambition, lustful passions and arrogance.** The Christian community must recognize the results of worldly attitudes and desires: disorder, quarrels, even murder. Prayers are too often offered for the wrong motives, while the wisdom from above is reasonable and merciful and makes for justice. Those who would be a friend of the sinful world are God's enemies. Yet God's grace is stronger than the spirit within us which turns toward evil.

The Gospel   Mark 9.30–37

In the Gospel **Jesus foretells his death and resurrection as the Son of Man, bids his disciples to have a servant ministry, and to learn to welcome him and God in a child.** The several sayings are linked together by the theme of Jesus' lowliness and readiness to suffer for others. His followers' difficulty in understanding him and their discussion concerning which of them is greatest stand in sharp contrast to their Lord's teachings. Jesus' action and words with regard to the child remind us of another saying: that whatever is done to the least member of the community is done to him.

For an introduction to a longer first lesson, Wisdom 1.16–2.1, 6–22, see p. 222.

171

PROPER TWENTY
(Sunday closest to September 21)

First Lesson   Amos 8.4–7

The Old Testament lesson is **a judgment on social injustice and religious hypocrisy.** During celebrations like the New Moon and Sabbaths no work was allowed. Yet traders were so full of greed that they only mechanically observed the festivals and could not wait for them to be over so that they might again swindle the poor. Such offences are also sins against the Lord, and he will not forget them.

Psalm 138: A hymn of praise and thanksgiving to the Lord on high, who has saved God's servant and cares for the lowly.

Second Lesson (The Epistle)   I Timothy 2.1–8

In this lesson **disciples are called upon to pray for all, including political rulers, so that Christians may lead peaceable and moral lives. It is God's will that everyone should find salvation.** Jesus is the mediator between the one God and humanity; he has sacrificed himself for the freedom of all. Paul has been appointed an apostle to make his saving work known to the Gentiles. During this period the newly-born Christian movement was a tiny part of society which felt that it needed peaceful conditions to spread its gospel. It usually took a positive view of the functions of the state in maintaining peace and justice.

The Gospel   Luke 16.1–13

Our Gospel is **the story of the steward who, when dismissed for mismanagement, showed himself to be very shrewd. This is followed by teaching about Mammon, that is, worldly wealth.** The joke would be on us if we fastened on the details of the story. The man's obviously dishonest behavior forces us to look more deeply for what is admirable about him—his readiness to face up to reality, together with his unquenchable hopefulness in the face of calamity. This is to be the attitude of Jesus' followers as the kingdom with its time of challenge and judgment approaches. The teaching on money suggests that disciples must know its significance, while never serving it.

For a longer first lesson, Amos 8.4–12, see p. 223.

PROPER TWENTY-ONE
(Sunday closest to September 28)

First Lesson   Ezekiel 18.1–4, 25–32

In the Old Testament lesson **the Lord insists that individuals are responsible for their own sins and that the people must now repent, no longer blaming their troubles on the sins of their parents.** So much for the proverb that the fathers have eaten sour grapes and the children's teeth are set on edge! So much for those who say the Lord's ways are not just! These words are intended to bring about a sense of individual responsibility and hope at a time when the nation was gripped by despair because of tribulation and exile. The Lord wants the people to turn away from iniquity and live.

Psalm 25.1–14 (or 3–9): A prayer for forgiveness and guidance and an expression of trust in the Lord.

Second Lesson (The Epistle)   Philippians 2.1–13

In this reading **Paul bids the new disciples to be of one mind in love, knowing how Christ Jesus accepted the condition of a servant and was obedient to the point of death. We now confess him as Lord and are called to an obedient working out of our faith.** Central to this passage is a poem which may have been adapted from the hopes for a savior of a people who did not yet know Jesus. He has fulfilled humanity's dream of one who will share fully in the mortal condition. Now the Lord is known personally—Jesus. His followers must work out their salvation while discovering that God is active in them for God's loving purpose.

The Gospel   Matthew 21.28–32

In the Gospel **Jesus tells a parable of two sons who obeyed their father differently, and he indicates that it is the same with those who are apparently obedient and disobedient in this age.** Both John the Baptist and Jesus offered their message of repentance and the hope of the reign of God to all. It was the religious outcasts who most genuinely responded. Then and now it is not a popular idea to suggest that such persons have priority over those who are established in their religion. Action is the test of obedience.

PROPER TWENTY-ONE
(Sunday closest to September 28)

First Lesson   Numbers 11.4–6, 10–16, 24–29

In our Old Testament story **the people weep and complain in the wilderness, and the Lord comes to Moses' help by sharing some of the prophet's spirit of leadership with seventy chosen elders and also with two others who were left behind in the camp.** This spirit manifests itself in temporary spells of ecstatic prophecy. The narrative has several interwoven themes. Once more God turns away wrath at Israel's lack of trust. The story is meant to show that all leadership derives its authority from Moses' God-given power. That the Spirit also falls on Eldad and Medad illustrates how it cannot be confined by human appointment.

Psalm 19 (or 19.7–14): A hymn which glorifies the Creator God, with special praise for God's law and a prayer for avoidance of sin.

Second Lesson (The Epistle)   James 4.7–12

In this lesson **Christians are counseled to purify themselves and to draw near to the Lord in penitence, while not presuming to judge their neighbors.** If disciples will stand up to the devil with his temptations, he will go away. God will then come close as we come near to God. While our condition of sin must lead to mourning, God raises us up. Finally, those who judge their neighbors make themselves judges above the law. God is the only judge and lawgiver.

The Gospel   Mark 9.38–43, 45, 47–48

In the Gospel **Jesus bids his disciples to accept all who seek to do good in his name and to deal ruthlessly with whatever part of themselves causes sin.** Early Christians were doubtless faced with people outside their communities who claimed they were acting in Christ's name. The tolerant answer given here suggests that Jesus' followers must avoid arrogance and be open to God acting as God wills. On the other hand, it is a serious matter to lead a believer astray. The counsel to destroy offending parts of the body is exaggerated to make clear the importance of avoiding various sins. The description of hell is drawn from the garbage dump outside Jerusalem.

For a longer second lesson, James 4.7–5.6, see p. 223.

174

PROPER TWENTY-ONE
(Sunday closest to September 28)

First Lesson   Amos 6.1–7

In the first reading **the prophet pronounces woe upon the proud and complacent leaders of Judah and Israel.** Now they spend their time in comfort and luxury. But they are no stronger than the cities of Syria or the Philistines. Amos made his stern prophecy because of the moral corruption in Israel over seven hundred years before the time of Christ. Shortly afterwards Israel was conquered by Assyria.

Psalm 146 (or 146.1–9): A hymn or praise to the Lord who forms the
world and rules in justice, and who heals and cares for the needy.

Second Lesson (The Epistle)   I Timothy 6.11–19

In this lesson **Paul exhorts Timothy to be strong with virtues in the race of faith, waiting for the appearance of the Lord Jesus. He is to instruct the rich to be generous and to store up the treasure of true life.** Timothy was one of Paul's trusted associates. Paul refers to his noble confession of faith and now charges Timothy, in the presence of God and of Jesus who made his testimony before Pontius Pilate, to keep the commandment with purity. Jesus will appear at the time appointed by the great Ruler and Lord, the immortal God, whom no mortal can ever see.

The Gospel   Luke 16.19–31

Our Gospel is **the story of the life and death of a rich man at whose gate lay a poor beggar by the name of Lazarus.** In the next life their situations are strikingly reversed. The rich man wishes that Lazarus could return to life to warn his brothers of the fate that awaits them. He is told, however, that if they do not heed Moses and the prophets, they will not listen even if someone rises from the dead. This last comment hints that there will continue to be a callousness toward the poor even after Jesus' resurrection. The story strongly suggests that now is the time that an irrevocable decision must be made.

PROPER TWENTY-TWO
(Sunday closest to October 5)

First Lesson   Isaiah 5.1–7

In our opening lesson **the prophet sings a sad parable about God's vineyard, Israel, and the destruction which must now come upon it.** Despite all God's loving care, this vineyard brought forth only sour grapes. The Lord looked for right judgment and found wrong. God hoped for justice and instead heard cries of distress.

Psalm 80 (or 80.7–14): A lament and a plea to the Lord, the shepherd of Israel, that the Lord will restore God's ravaged vineyard.

Second Lesson (The Epistle)   Philippians 3.14–21

In this reading **Paul urges the Philippian disciples to follow his example in pressing on toward the goal of God's call, watching out for those who are conformed to worldly ways, while expecting the deliverance of Jesus who will transform this mortal body into a body like his own.** Paul had earlier warned of the dangers of false teachers who insist on circumcision as a requirement necessary for salvation. He has told his own story of conversion from dependence on a legalistic understanding of religion to faith in Jesus. Now he weeps bitter tears over those whose minds are dominated by perishable matters. The disciples, by contrast, are on the way toward the realization of a heavenly citizenship.

The Gospel   Matthew 21.33–43

Our Gospel is **the story of the wicked and disloyal tenants who are cast out of the vineyard.** The parable is presented to us as an allegory in which the vineyard is Israel and the wicked tenants are its people. The servants sent to them are the prophets, and the son whom they kill is Jesus. To the hearing of the early church the destruction of the vineyard would parallel the destruction of Jerusalem by the Romans in 70 A.D., while the heritage of the vineyard is now given to others. There is added an ancient prophecy concerning the stone which was rejected, but which has now become the main cornerstone for the Lord's new work.

176

PROPER TWENTY-TWO
(Sunday closest to October 5)

First Lesson   Genesis 2.18–24

The Old Testament lesson tells **the story of the creation of woman to be a companion with man after God had made the animals and the man had named them.** The first human is shown to be superior to all other creatures by his power of language. But he still has no partner. So God shapes woman from his rib, and together they are a common humanity; they are "one flesh." Man leaves his own family to share life with woman in an innocence where sexuality is a source of neither embarrassment nor contention.

Psalm 8: The psalmist glorifies the Lord, sovereign of the earth and the magnificent heavens, who has made human life to have mastery over all other earthly creatures. **Or** Psalm 128: The one who reveres the Lord will be blessed with many children, a long life and the prosperity of Jerusalem.

Second Lesson (The Epistle)   Hebrews 2.9–18

In this lesson we learn how **Jesus has shared fully in all that it means to be human and, as our leader and high priest, is able to help us in our temptations.** Only by experiencing death himself could he break the power of death over us. Clearly this was not done for the benefit of angels (of which the author has just spoken) but for the descendants of Abraham. Made of flesh and blood, participating in our sufferings and temptations, Jesus has become the perfect and merciful high priest so that our sins may be forgiven.

The Gospel   Mark 10.2–9

In the Gospel **Jesus is asked about divorce, and he reaches back to the creation story to set before his hearers the ideal of the marriage relationship.** In Jesus' lifetime there were many views held about divorce, some stricter, some more lenient. In one sense, Jesus is the most strict of all: what through natural union God has made one cannot be separated by human action. Yet, in another sense, Jesus' answer refuses to deal with the question in the way it is asked. Instead he honors the solemnity and purpose of marriage. The motivation for Jesus' words may have been his concern with men who set aside their wives and, in that society, left them poor and insecure.

For a longer second lesson, Hebrews 2.1–18, see p. 223.

PROPER TWENTY-TWO
(Sunday closest to October 5)

First Lesson   Habakkuk 1.1–6, 12–13; 2.1–4

In our first reading **the prophet bitterly complains to the Lord about the injustice and violence in the world. God answers that justice will come in time; meanwhile, the righteous will live by faithfulness and loyalty.** It is the time of the Chaldean (or Babylonian) invasion. Habakkuk cannot understand how God can allow all this evil and destruction. He takes his position in the watchtower to await the Lord's reply. Those who are right with God will continue to live by their trust in God.

Psalm 37.1–18 (or 3–10): A psalm of advice to the wise, instructing them to avoid evil and to wait patiently on the Lord in righteousness. The Lord will cut off the wicked.

Second Lesson (The Epistle)   II Timothy 1.1–5

This passage is **the opening of Paul's letter to his friend and co-worker Timothy.** He keeps him always in his prayers and remembers his faith. Timothy was the son of a Jewish mother and a Gentile father who became a companion of Paul's at a relatively young age.

The Gospel   Luke 17.5–10

In the Gospel lesson **Jesus tells his disciples of faith's great power, and reminds them that servants must not expect special privileges or thanks merely for doing their duty.** The first saying forcefully stresses the realization that faith's strength—even the power of a little faith—ought never be underestimated. The story about the hard working servant and the master makes the point that humans can never hold any claim over God and put God in their debt. For Jesus' followers there is no room for boasting or self-righteousness because of their faith and service.

For introductions to longer first and second lessons, Habakkuk 1.1–13; 2.1–4 and II Timothy 1.1–14, see p. 224.

178

PROPER TWENTY-THREE
(Sunday closest to October 12)

First Lesson   Isaiah 25.1–9

In our Old Testament lesson **the prophet praises the Lord for destroying the cities of the ruthless and for providing a refuge for the poor. Now comes the banquet of the Lord's salvation.** God is the ultimate source of security. The great feast takes place on the mountain of the Lord's temple, Mount Zion, where heaven and earth figuratively meet. The banquet will be for all people, and even the power of death will be overcome.

Psalm 23: The Lord is shepherd and guide. God is present in time of danger and spreads a table for the one who needs comfort.

Second Lesson (The Epistle)   Philippians 4.4–13

In his letter to the church at Philippi, Paul invites the new disciples to exult in joy in the Lord who is near at hand, and he thanks them for their most recent gift. They need have no anxiety because God's peace, which is beyond human understanding, will keep their hearts and thoughts in Jesus. They should fill their minds with all that is noble and loving, putting these things into practice as Paul has taught them to do. This is the only church from which Paul accepted support. Without slighting their kindness, he wants them to know that he has found the strength to be satisfied in all kinds of circumstances.

The Gospel   Matthew 22.1–14

Our Gospel reading presents **a parable about those who declined invitations to a marriage feast and others who were then invited, followed by the story of a guest who came without wedding clothes.** As the evangelist presents the parable of the feast it is an allegory about the rejection of the Jews and the acceptance of Gentiles into the kingdom. At another level, the story suggests that God's kingdom will become known whether people are prepared for it or not. It is his gift. Included will be all kinds of people, many of them not considered worthy by worldly standards. The second parable, originally a separate story, makes the point that one must be ready for the kingdom at all times; the invitation comes unexpectedly.

179

PROPER TWENTY-THREE
(Sunday closest to October 12)

First Lesson   Amos 5.6–7, 10–15

In our opening reading **the prophet denounces corruption and injustice, but offers hope to the survivors of the impending destruction if they will seek the Lord and love good while hating evil.** God's judgment will be like fire on all the iniquities of the people of the northern kingdom in Palestine. They will not live to enjoy their ill-gotten luxury. The prudent individual will be shocked into silence.

Psalm 90 (or 90.1–8, 12): The psalmist reflects on the passing character of human life in the face of the Lord's wrath and asks the everlasting God for wisdom to make use of the time.

Second Lesson (The Epistle)   Hebrews 3.1–6

In this New Testament lesson **Jesus, as God's messenger and the faithful high priest, is shown to be far greater than Moses, as a son of the house is superior to a servant.** Throughout this part of his letter, the author seeks to show Jesus' supremacy over various Old Testament figures and institutions: Moses, Joshua, the Jewish high priesthood, law and covenants, even angels. All these have their significance in pointing to Jesus. The author here argues in the style of the times. Moses is called God's servant in the scriptures, but Jesus is known as God's Son. He is set over God's whole household, that is, over us, if we keep fast to our hope.

The Gospel   Mark 10.17–27

In the Gospel **Jesus counsels a would-be disciple to give all to the poor and follow him. He then teaches his disciples how hard it is for those with riches to enter the kingdom.** Jesus first refuses to let himself be called *good* since that description belongs to God alone. He then finds that the man has tried to live out his duties toward his neighbor in response to divine love. But the decision for discipleship must go beyond this. If the heart is divided by desires for worldly security, there is no way one can enter into the kingdom's loving justice. Yet by the power of God people can be converted and saved.

For a longer version of the Gospel lesson, Mark 10.17–31, see p. 224.

PROPER TWENTY-THREE
(Sunday closest to October 12)

First Lesson   Ruth 1.8–19a

Our opening lesson tells of **Ruth's decision to leave her own country and return with her mother-in-law Naomi to Israel.** Naomi's husband and two sons die while living in Moab. Ruth persists in her desire to go back to Bethlehem with Naomi and to accept Israel's God as her own. Later she will marry a relative of her father-in-law and, though a foreign woman, become the grandmother of King David. The narrative is both a touching lesson of loyalty and devotion and an illustration that God's ways of bringing about divine purposes often differ from human expectations.

Psalm 113: Praise to the Lord enthroned on high who lifts up the weak and lowly. God makes the barren woman a joyful mother.

Second Lesson (The Epistle)   II Timothy 2.8–15

In this reading **Paul bids Timothy to be a faithful worker, reminding himself and others of Jesus' resurrection and the new life that is to be known with him.** Although Paul is shut up in prison, the gospel is free in the world. The apostle reflects on his own sufferings and encourages his younger associate in his role of leadership. Especially should he warn his people to avoid disputes over words. The verses which begin, "If we died with him, we shall live with him" seem part of an early Christian hymn.

The Gospel   Luke 17.11–19

In the Gospel story **Jesus' command brings about the cleansing of ten lepers, but only one, a Samaritan, returns to give thanks.** Jesus is on the way to his destiny in Jerusalem. The narrative illustrates the power of the reign of God to give a new lease on life. The lepers, who were formerly outcasts, would now be allowed to return home. But only a despised Samaritan recognizes that a life of gratitude and faith is now possible. Physical healing is but a first step. He becomes whole and finds salvation.

The first lesson may be lengthened to Ruth 1.1–19a, for which the introduction above is also suitable. For a longer second reading, II Timothy 2.3–15, see p. 225.

PROPER TWENTY-FOUR
(Sunday closest to October 19)

First Lesson   Isaiah 45.1–7

In our Old Testament reading **the Lord anoints Cyrus, King of Persia, to be God's agent in freeing the chosen people from exile.** The time is more than five centuries before the birth of Christ. The prophet perceives that God is working through a foreign king who does not even know the Lord. But God enables Cyrus to conquer over Babylonia and then to set Israel free. Boldly the prophet speaks in the Lord's name: the Creator is responsible for everything that happens in the world—all which seems a blessing and all disaster.

Psalm 96 (or 96.1–9): A song to the Lord, the Creator and Ruler of all nations, in which the whole world is invited to join.

Second Lesson (The Epistle)   I Thessalonians 1.1–10

In company with Silvanus and Timothy, Paul greets the new Christians of Thessalonica, gives thanks for their faith and their conversion from idols to the worship of the true and living God. This letter was written not long after Paul's first missionary visit to this city in the country we know today as Greece. Evidently the converts were all former pagans. The apostle refers to the troubles and persecution which are also reported in the Acts of the Apostles. But the gospel, empowered by the activity of the Holy Spirit, has inspired a faith which has become widely known.

The Gospel   Matthew 22.15–22

In our Gospel lesson **Jesus answers a question about taxation by teaching that people should pay what belongs to the Emperor to the Emperor and the things of God to God.** The question was meant as a trap. If Jesus advised the paying of taxes to the occupying Roman powers, many Jews would have considered him a collaborator. Had he counseled nonpayment, the Herodian servants of the Romans could accuse him of sedition. On one level Jesus' answer is a master-stroke of clever ambiguity, but it also causes his hearers to reflect more deeply on their responsibility to God and the State. Perhaps the saying suggests that government has its legitimate yet limited claims. It must not be given the highest allegiance.

PROPER TWENTY-FOUR
(Sunday closest to October 19)

First Lesson   Isaiah 53.4–12

Our opening lesson is **the poem of the Lord's servant who suffers and bears the sins of many.** The passage is part of the fourth and last of the "servant songs" which form a portion of the Book of Isaiah written when the exile was coming to an end. The servant is sometimes thought to be an historical individual or an idealization of the faithful of Israel. This "man of sorrows," "despised and rejected," "wounded for our transgressions," whom the Lord at last vindicates, is perceived by Christians to be a prefigurement of Jesus.

Psalm 91 (or 91.9–16): A hymn of trust in the Lord. God will guard and deliver the one who loves and seeks refuge with God.

Second Lesson (The Epistle)   Hebrews 4.12–16

This reading reminds us that **the Lord's word is active, probing the human heart and all creation, while we can yet boldly approach God's throne because Jesus, our great high priest, has known our weaknesses and temptations.** The first statement is a warning: God's word, which God has spoken at the creation, through the scriptures, and personally in Jesus, is everywhere and makes judgment. But we now have a heavenly high priest, our brother, who knows all about our life, and helps us to find God's mercy. The insistence that Jesus was without sin relies not on extensive knowledge of what he did not do, but on the memory of his positive dedication to God's will.

The Gospel   Mark 10.35–45

In the Gospel story **Jesus' followers still expect that his way will quickly lead to a state of glory in which they want special places. Jesus tells them of a different path of discipleship.** First Jesus and then his disciples must experience the cup of sorrow and the baptism of death. They are not to live and act like worldly rulers. They must lead in servanthood. Their example is Jesus who as the Son of Man serves and gives his life.

PROPER TWENTY-FOUR
(Sunday closest to October 19)

First Lesson   Genesis 32.3–8, 22–30

Our Old Testament reading tells how **Jacob, on the night before his confrontation with his brother Esau, wrestles all night with a figure he comes to recognize as God.** Many years earlier Jacob had tricked Esau and stolen his blessing and birthright. Now Jacob has grown rich in the service of his father-in-law Laban, but he greatly fears his meeting with his brother. Jacob's struggle with God may in part express his guilty conscience and coming to terms with the evil he had done. He has to fight for a blessing and permission to return to his homeland. For his new life he is given a new name, Israel, but is left with an injury as a sign of God's supremacy and a reminder of his wrong.

Psalm 121: A song of trust in the Lord, the unsleeping guardian of Israel.

Second Lesson (The Epistle)   II Timothy 3.14–4.5

In this lesson **Paul exhorts Timothy to continue calmly and diligently with his ministry, teaching from the scriptures and preaching the word of God.** The passage suggests a period in the life of the church when there were a number of teachers, who called themselves Christians, but who presented their own versions of the faith. Now is a time to stress the essentials. Timothy is urged to remain established in what he has been taught and in the scriptures, meaning here the writings of the Old Testament, which are useful for many forms of instruction.

The Gospel   Luke 18.1–8a

In our Gospel **Jesus tells a comic parable about a judge who was so pestered by a woman that he finally gave in to her pleas.** The evangelist tells the story in order to commend persistent prayer. It would be particularly appropriate at a time when the people were losing heart. An earlier focus of the parable was probably on the corrupt and impious judge. If even such a man as this will finally render justice, how much more will God hear those who call on God.

After Pentecost   Year A

PROPER TWENTY-FIVE
(Sunday closest to October 26)

First Lesson   Exodus 22.21–27

In the Old Testament lesson **Israel is called to a keen sense of justice and social responsibility toward the stranger, the widow and orphan, and the poor.** One must not use a loan to extract interest from those who are already in poverty. These injunctions are part of the people's covenant with God. The Israelites were themselves once strangers and sojourners until God showed them mercy.

Psalm 1: The Lord makes frutiful those who choose the way of righteousness.

Second Lesson (The Epistle)   1 Thessalonians 2.1–8

In this reading **Paul recalls his first visit to the Thessalonians, the troubles he endured, and the straightforward and gentle way in which he presented the gospel.** The opposition which Paul had earlier experienced in Philippi continued in Thessalonica but, with God's help, Paul preached fearlessly. Unlike certain of the insincere traveling missionaries of the pagan world, Paul acted with integrity and sought in no way to take advantage of his new friends. He and his companions shared not only the gospel but their own selves.

The Gospel   Matthew 22.34–46

In the Gospel **Jesus presents the double commandment of love for God and neighbor, and then asks a question concerning whose son the Christ is.** The context of this passage is the effort by certain Jewish officials to test Jesus, hoping to force him to make an unwise or unpopular comment. Jesus first responds by teaching that all the law and the prophetic words depend for their understanding on the commandments of love. He then asks his own question. Using an argumentative style of the time, Jesus shows how King David (considered to be the author of the Psalms) called the Christ his Lord. Thus, at the very least, the Christ must be more than the son of David. Christians believe this Christ to be Jesus and trust that through him disciples may learn to love both God and neighbor.

PROPER TWENTY-FIVE
(Sunday closest to October 26)

First Lesson   Isaiah 59.9–19

In the Old Testament lesson we hear **the people's lament: there is a lack of righteousness in the land; injustice is everywhere. Soon the Lord will come as a mighty warrior to bring retribution.** Darkness now reigns over the nation and sin multiplies. Truth goes unspoken. But in this time of iniquity God puts on his armor of righteousness. All will learn to fear the Lord.

Psalm 13: The psalmist laments the absence of the Lord, but still continues to trust in God.

Second Lesson (The Epistle)   Hebrews 5.12–6.1, 9–12

In this reading **some early Christians are chastised for their lack of growth in the faith, but are then encouraged in the hope of salvation if they pursue it eagerly.** The problem with these disciples is neither immorality nor wrong belief but a lazy inattentiveness. It is embarrassing that grown people must still be bottle-fed on the basic subjects of belief. God, however, will not forget the good they have done, and they may yet become like those who through faith and patience are inheriting the promises.

The Gospel   Mark 10.46–52

Our Gospel is **the story of the new vision of blind Bartimaeus.** The evangelist has carefully prepared for this story by illustrating the inability of the religious officials to perceive who Jesus is and by describing the shortsightedness of the disciples. Now, with nothing but his great hope, this blind beggar calls out to Jesus. He uses the only title of honor he can think of—Son of David, dangerous words in the present political climate. But Jesus stops on his own profound journey, and Bartimaeus is healed through his faith. Then, as a model of a disciple who has received healing as a gift, he follows Jesus on the way to suffering and death before glory.

For an introduction to a longer version of the first lesson, Isaiah 59.1–4, 9–19, see p. 225.

186

PROPER TWENTY-FIVE
(Sunday closest to October 26)

First Lesson   Jeremiah 14.7–10, 19–22

In the Old Testament reading **the people bitterly lament their sins. They are troubled by a great drought; the Lord is far from them and determined to punish them for their iniquities.** Is God like a stranger passing through the land? Is God powerless to help? Despite all the people's wrongdoings, will the Lord not honor the temple where God's name dwells? Will God forget the covenant?

Psalm 84 (or 84.1–6): A song of the pilgrims' happiness as they come to worship in the house of the Lord. In the desolate valleys they will find springs of water.

Second Lesson (The Epistle)   II Timothy 4.6–8, 16–18

In this passage **Paul, believing that his death is near, closes his letter to Timothy and looks forward with great faith to the heavenly kingdom.** Paul is in prison in Rome, having already been put on trial once and barely escaping the lion's jaws. Although he may only be speaking figuratively, some form of martyrdom appears close at hand. Even his friends have deserted him. Still he proclaims the gospel and is ready to be sacrificed, trusting that the Lord will soon appear. His perseverance becomes a pillar for the continuing faith of the church.

The Gospel   Luke 18.9–14

Our Gospel lesson is **the story of the Pharisee who trusts in his righteousness and the sinful tax collector.** The parable illustrates repeated themes of the Gospels: God's ways frequently reverse human expectations. It is God's acceptance and not human merit which opens the gift of the kingdom.

It will be helpful if the reader begins verses 7 and 19 of the first lesson with some phrase such as "The people lament." This first lesson may be lengthened to Jeremiah 14.1–10, 19–22. The introduction above is also suitable for the longer reading.

PROPER TWENTY-SIX
(Sunday closest to November 2)

First Lesson   Micah 3.5–12

Our first lesson is **a denunciation of professional prophets who suit their oracles to whatever gain they get.** So long as they are fed they speak only of peace and never challenge the status quo, while yet they threaten those who give them nothing. It shall be like night on these prophets, with only silence from God. But Micah's words of judgment on all the corrupt leaders of Jerusalen will come to pass. No protection will be found in saying "The Lord is with us." Although Jerusalem avoided the Assyrian devastation in Micah's lifetime, one hundred years later it became a heap of ruins just as he prophesied.

Psalm 43: A plea to God, by one who is persecuted and in distress, to be able to come and worship in the Lord's temple.

Second Lesson (The Epistle)   I Thessalonians 2.9–13, 17–20

In this reading **Paul defends his ministry among the Thessalonians and regrets his inability to visit them again, while still they remain his joy and glory.** Paul may have heard some criticism. Perhaps it was said that he was unwilling to return out of fear of persecution. Ever sensitive, Paul responds that he has been hindered by the kind of difficulties which Satan devises. He reminds his converts how solicitous he was in presenting the gospel and how hard he worked for his own living in order not be a burden on them.

The Gospel   Matthew 23.1–12

In the Gospel **Jesus decries religious officials who tie burdens on others, while themselves delighting in honors and flattery. Disciples are to lead a very different way of life.** The leaders of the time possess Moses' authority, and their teaching should be regarded as valid. But their practice is out of keeping. Members of the Christian community are not to set themselves up over each other. There are to be no honorific titles such as revered teacher, father or master. The greatest must act as servant.

PROPER TWENTY-SIX
(Sunday closest to November 2)

First Lesson   Deuteronomy 6.1–9

In our opening reading **Moses tells the people that they must carefully keep the ten commandments which he has just given them.** This is the Lord's covenant, for, if Israel will observe these statutes, then all will go well with them in their new land. They shall teach them to their children and, as signs of their devotion, wear little boxes with passages of scripture in them. Central to Israel's faith is the *Shema* which every Jew is to recite daily, and which begins: "Hear, O Israel: the Lord our God is one Lord." He shall be wholly loved. The Lord's claim upon Israel is total.

Psalm 119.1–16 (or 1–8): Happy are those who walk in the law of the Lord, who guide their ways by God's commandments.

Second Lesson (The Epistle)   Hebrews 7.23–28

In this New Testament lesson **the author demonstrates how Jesus is our perfect and everlasting high priest.** He was appointed not by men according to the law, but by an oath of God. He had no need to offer sacrifices for his own sins, for he is holy and undefiled. Nor does he offer sacrifices repeatedly, but once for all he presented the perfect sacrifice of himself. His priesthood is forever and, as the Son, he now makes eternal intercession for us.

The Gospel   Mark 12.28–34

In the Gospel **Jesus answers a question concerning the chief command of the law by reciting the double commandment to love God and one's neighbor.** Jesus was not unique in bringing together these two great teachings from Israel's heritage, but the New Testament gives them special emphasis. They are closely linked, for, in responding to God's love, we learn that we are lovable, and so begin to be able to love others as ourselves. In loving our neighbors we discover the mystery that we are also loving in them their Creator. The man who asked Jesus the question repeats the commandments in his own words. He is not far from the kingdom.

189

PROPER TWENTY-SIX
(Sunday closest to November 2)

First Lesson   Isaiah 1.10–20

Our opening lesson tells how **the Lord cannot abide the offerings and solemn ceremonies of a people who are without compassion and bloody with injustice. Yet, if they turn from their ways and become obedient, God will wash them clean.** Otherwise they will die. Judah's rulers and people are so corrupt that they are compared to the notorious cities of Sodom and Gomorrah.

Psalm 32 (or 32.1–8): A thanksgiving for the forgiveness of sin.

Second Lesson (The Epistle)   II Thessalonians 1.1–5, 11–12

Together with Silvanus and Timothy, Paul greets the new disciples in Thessalonica. He offers thanks to God for the increase of their faith under persecution and assures them of his prayers. Paul is so proud of their growing faith and love that he boasts about them to others. He suggests that their present troubles may be God's way of proving them worthy of the reign of God.

The Gospel   Luke 19.1–10

Our Gospel is **the story of Jesus' acceptance of Zacchaeus, the tax-collector, and the transformation of his life.** This is an enacted parable about the power of forgiveness and acceptance to create emotional and spiritual healing. Tax gatherers became rich through extortion and were despised by their own countrymen and the Romans under whom they served. Here Jesus demonstrates his own conviction that the opportunity of the kingdom is open to all. He glimpses Zacchaeus' hope for a different kind of life in his child-like act of climbing into the sycamore tree, and he offers to share Zacchaeus' hospitality.

For an introduction to a longer second lesson, II Thessalonians 1.1–12, see p. 225.

PROPER TWENTY-SEVEN
(Sunday closest to November 9)

First Lesson   Amos 5.18–24

In our Old Testament lesson **the prophet proclaims that the day of the Lord will be a day of deep gloom. God despises the ceremonies of his people and calls for a continuous stream of justice and righteousness.** In this era people looked forward to "the day of the Lord" as an annual time of festival and also a symbol of the great final day when God would make all things well. How wrong they are! It will be a day of darkness, not light. No matter where one turns disaster awaits. The Lord is done with rites without righteousness, and religiosity as a substitute for equity.

Psalm 70: A prayer for help and vindication.

Second Lesson (The Epistle)   I Thessalonians 4.13–18

In this reading **Paul offers a vision of how the dead in Christ will rise and then, together with those who are alive, be caught up to meet the Lord in the sky.** Apparently some members of the Thessalonian church had died, and there was this concern: would they miss the Lord's coming? First, Paul reminds them that the Christian hope is rooted in the God who raised Jesus. He then describes the day of the Lord's appearing and the raising up of the dead and the living, using highly poetic imagery conditioned by the world view of his time. The essential meaning is clear: we shall be with the Lord.

The Gospel   Matthew 25.1–13

Our Gospel is **the parable of the wise and foolish maidens— those prepared and unprepared for the bridegroom's coming.** In several ways the details of the story may strike us as odd and even a little unfair, but such a concern misses the main point which has much in common with other of Jesus' parables. One must at all times be ready with repentance and decision for the kingdom's coming. In a later period this story was read with allegorical overtones. Jesus is the bridegroom whose return is delayed. Some in the church are falling asleep while others remain expectant.

PROPER TWENTY-SEVEN
(Sunday closest to November 9)

First Lesson   I Kings 17.8–16

From the Old Testament we hear **the story of the food which God miraculously provided for the prophet Elijah and the widow of Zarephath and her family.** There is famine throughout the land which Elijah has prophesied because of the sinfulness of King Ahab. The story shows that God is present to care for God's prophet and also for this woman who, though a foreigner, has shared with Elijah what little she has. The word of the Lord is powerful to fulfill its promise even beyond the borders of Israel.

Psalm 146 (or 146.4–9): A hymn to the Lord who forms the world and rules in justice, who heals and cares for the orphan and widow.

Second Lesson (The Epistle)   Hebrews 9.24–28

This reading tells how **Christ, the eternal high priest, has entered into the heavenly sanctuary to present the ultimate and perfect sacrifice of himself for sins.** It is the author's theme that Jesus has superseded the need for all other priestly offerings such as were made annually on the Day of Atonement. These were never more than foreshadowings of what Christ was to accomplish. The earthly temple, which was but a copy of the true sanctuary in heaven, is no longer of significance. As the end of the age draws near, our brother Jesus, who died like we must, appears before God on our behalf and will appear once more to save those who wait for him.

The Gospel   Mark 12.38–44

In the Gospel lesson **Jesus warns against religious officials who love honors and flattery, and he then points out a poor widow who makes an offering of what little she possesses.** Together the two stories stress a theme found often in the Gospels: those who think themselves religious are in great danger of living a life of hypocrisy, while genuine trust in God may be found among the least obvious. The religious officials take advantage of people like widows, and wealthy persons make a show of giving large sums of money, but the woman herself is an example of the greatest generosity. Her gift of all she has points forward to Jesus' self-offering.

PROPER TWENTY-SEVEN
(Sunday closest to November 9)

First Lesson   Job 19.23–27a

In our Old Testament lesson **the deeply troubled Job continues to struggle with the injustices which affect his life. He trusts one day he will be vindicated.** Job believes he has lived decently and honestly. Yet every misfortune imaginable has befallen him. Neither his friends nor God can give him a satisfactory reason for his troubles. That is why he wishes his plea to be lastingly engraved in stone and trusts that God will at last be his defender.

Psalm 17 (or 17.1–8): A plea for justice and protection by one who has followed God's ways.

Second Lesson (The Epistle)   II Thessalonians 2.13–3.5

In this reading **Paul gives thanks for the Thessalonian converts whom God has called to salvation, and he urges them to stand firm in the traditions he has taught them and in the good works which the Lord encourages them to do.** Paul had earlier instructed these disciples that there must be a fierce struggle between good and evil before the coming of the Lord. He asks for their prayers that the word of God may rapidly spread abroad and that Paul himself may be kept safe from wrong-headed and wicked persons.

The Gospel   Luke 20.27, 34–38

In the Gospel **the Sadducees ask a question about the resurrection. Jesus replies that resurrection means a different existence from earthly life, and that it depends on a God who has a personal and living relationship with all people.** The Sadducees did not believe in resurrection from death, and they attempted to make it seem absurd by asking what would then be the legal situation for a person who had been married several times. Jesus cuts through their apparent cleverness. There is no need for marriage after the resurrection. What is more, the Bible continues to speak of the patriarchs as though they were still alive before God.

For an introduction to a longer version of the Gospel, Luke 20.27–38, see p. 226.

193

PROPER TWENTY-EIGHT
(Sunday closest to November 16)

First Lesson   Zephaniah 1.7, 12–18

In the opening lesson **the prophet proclaims the hastening approach of the day of the Lord, a day of judgment and fearful distress.** Zephaniah calls for silence as the Lord prepares what will be a sacrifice of terror. Everywhere in Judah there is corruption. People are drunk with wine and say that the Lord will do nothing, nothing either good or bad. But they will never enjoy their wealth, nor will their silver or gold be of any use. The portrayal of the end is vivid and terrifying.

Psalm 90 (or 90.1–8, 12): The psalmist reflects on the passing character of human life in the face of the Lord's wrath, and asks the everlasting God for wisdom to make use of the time.

Second Lesson (The Epistle)   I Thessalonians 5.1–10

In this reading **Paul counsels the new disciples to be alert as in the daylight, for the day of the Lord will come swiftly and unexpectedly, although at a time unknown to mortals.** Many early Christians believed that the course of world history would soon come to an end. Paul urges the Thessalonians not to live like people of the night, but soberly and expectantly. Whether they first die or remain alive they may look forward, not to God's wrath, but to a salvation that has been gained through Jesus. Paul's central point remains valid for us: we do not know when the consummation of history will take place, but are to live always prepared for judgment.

The Gospel   Matthew 25.14–15, 19–29

Our Gospel is **the parable of the servants who made different uses of the money entrusted to them.** The evangelist intends the story to be instructive to Christian disciples. The master Jesus is now away. When he returns, he will expect his followers to have made diligent use of the faith he has left in their charge. If it has not grown, then it has been without value and will be taken away. One also recognizes how immense are the sums left with the servants. The parable warns against the false security of only guarding the traditions and not investing them in life and in others.

194

PROPER TWENTY-EIGHT
(Sunday closest to November 16)

First Lesson   Daniel 12.1–4a

In our Old Testament lesson **Daniel is given a vision of the end of human history: after a period of great distress, some will be brought to their salvation and others to eternal disgrace.** This was a time of persecution for Israel which took place two centuries before the life of Christ. This oracle of hope makes use of imagery common to apocalyptic visions. Evil will mount up in a last desperate effort before Michael, Israel's patron angel, intervenes to bring justice. The names of all who will be saved are written in the book of life which must for now remain sealed. In what is a new idea for Judaism, even the faithful dead will be raised to receive their reward.

Psalm 16 (or 16.5–11): Contentment, refuge and joy are found in the presence of the Lord. To the faithful one, God will show the path of life.

Second Lesson (The Epistle)   Hebrews 10.31–39

In this reading **a community of Christians is warned of God's judgment and is encouraged not to shrink back but to endure in the faith that God will soon make salvation known.** These disciples had apparently already experienced considerable tribulation. Now they are in danger of complacency. The author had earlier told them of the severity of the penalty for those who learned the truth but went on sinning. Further persecution may be just around the corner; yet they must continue steadfast in doing God's will.

The Gospel   Mark 13.14–23

In the Gospel **the disciples are forewarned of an act of sacrilege, a time of fearful tribulation, and the appearance of persons claiming to be the Christ.** Many Jews and early Christians believed that the forces of evil would wage a last desperate battle before the end of history. In one sense it is a way of saying that evil makes it strongest challenge just when the opportunity for good is the greatest. This oracle was used to help interpret the meaning of events a generation or so after Christ's death. The desolating sacrilege was a pagan profanation of the temple. The Lord will make the struggle mercifully short.

For a longer first lesson, Daniel 12.1–4a, 5–13, see p. 226.

195

PROPER TWENTY-EIGHT
(Sunday closest to November 16)

First Lesson   Malachi 3.13–4.2a, 5–6

Our Old Testament reading tells of **the Lord's judgment: the wicked will be burned away, while the healing sun will rise on those who reverence the Lord. But before that day, the prophet Elijah will come to seek to reconcile.** It is a time when many are uncertain and doubt God's justice. Yet the Lord is watching, and soon will make clear the distinction between the good and the bad. Since the saying about Elijah's return was the last prophetic oracle of the Hebrew Bible, it had profound influence upon later Jewish and Christian thinking. Some early Christians believed that John the Baptist or possibly Jesus might be this figure of reconciliation.

Psalm 98 (or 98.5–10): A song of thanksgiving and praise to the victorious Lord who has made righteousness known and shown faithfulness to the people of God.

Second Lesson (The Epistle)   II Thessalonians 3.6–13

In this lesson **Paul deals with the problem of those who are so expectant that the Lord will come soon and are so meddlesome in the affairs of others that they have given up their daily work.** These individuals may have believed that they were already exalted to such a spiritual plane that mundane matters were no longer a concern for them. This may seem like piety on their part, but it means they have become a problem for others. Paul reminds them of his own example and bluntly rules that such people should either work or else not eat.

The Gospel   Luke 21.5–19

In the Gospel passage **the disciples are forewarned of the destruction of the Jewish temple and of great upheavals in the natural and supernatural order which must take place before the end of history.** There will be persecutions and divisions in families. Individuals will appear claiming to be Jesus. While in some passages the New Testament suggests that the end and fulfillment of human time will come quite unexpectedly, here the disciples are advised of a period of great tribulation when the powers of evil will make their final onslaught. In one sense this is poetic language used to describe the undescribable, but it insists that the ultimate meaning of life will finally be known.

PROPER TWENTY-NINE
(Sunday closest to November 23)

First Lesson   Ezekiel 34.11–17

In our opening reading **the Lord promises to be the shepherd of the people.** God will bring them home and heal them. God will feed and protect them. The exile of Israel is coming to an end. Ezekiel has prophesied against the false shepherds, the rulers who only fed off the flock. Now God will tend the sheep who have been dispersed and preyed upon, but the overfed will be judged.

Psalm 95.1–7: A call to worship the great God and Ruler, Creator of all the earth. We are his sheep, the people of God's pasture.

Second Lesson (The Epistle)   I Corinthians 15.20–28

In this lesson **Paul describes the plan of the resurrection age: it has begun with Christ's rising from the dead and will be fulfilled when all things are subjected to God.** Some of the Corinthians either doubted Christ's resurrection or held that Christians could already live a fully resurrected life of the spirit without any regard for the body. Paul insists on the reality of Christ's rising which has made possible the hope of new life in a world where all presently die a death like Adam's. Now the ascended Christ rules, winning his battles over the forces of evil, death being his final victim. All will culminate as God no longer reigns indirectly through Christ but becomes known everywhere as Lord over all.

The Gospel   Matthew 25.31–46

Our Gospel presents **a picture of the universal judgment when the Son of Man, acting as judge and ruler, will separate humankind into two groups: those who have cared for the Lord in the needy, the stranger and prisoners—and those who have not.** On one level the evangelist intends those in need to be understood as Christian disciples. But the bringing of all peoples into judgment has caused Christians to realize that the Christ is to be recognized in every individual. Beneath this awareness lies a profound theological mystery: the likeness of God, which has been decisively revealed in the human person of Jesus, may be perceived in each human being.

PROPER TWENTY-NINE
(Sunday closest to November 23)

First Lesson   Daniel 7.9–14

With striking imagery this reading presents **a scene of judgment in heaven and a vision of one like a son of man coming to rule in an everlasting kingdom.** The ancient figure is God, and the one who appears like a human seems to be symbolic of the future people of Israel. The imagery derives from pre-Israelite mythology and once was used to picture the beginning of a reign of a new ruler. Christians later understood the vision to be a prefigurement of Jesus' exaltation and role in judgment as the divine Son of Man.

Psalm 93: God reigns, the Lord of all creation. God has established the earth and subdued the great waters.

Second Lesson   Revelation 1.1–8

In this lesson **the Revelation made known to a disciple named John begins with a greeting from the everlasting God, from the seven spirits which worship God, and from Jesus Christ, the first-born from the dead.** The series of visions which follow are sent to seven churches, a sacred number which throughout this book signifies completion. Jesus, who continues to love his disciples, is praised as the faithful witness whose sacrifice has formed a royal household, a new priestly people to serve God. Soon he will come, like the one foreseen by the prophet Daniel, on the clouds of heaven. He now rules over all earthly kings, and God, the Alpha and Omega, the first and the last, is sovereign over all.

The Gospel   John 18.33–37

In the Gospel, **as his passion draws near, Jesus comes face to face with the Roman governor, and seeks to explain the nature of his kingship.** It has been suggested to Pilate that Jesus pretends to be some form of political ruler. But Jesus' kingship does not use the force of this world's weapons. Pilate then realizes that Jesus' kingship must be of a different order. The sovereignty of Jesus is found in his witness to divine truth. He reveals God's purpose and character, and those who share in this truth hear his voice.

For an alternative Gospel reading, Mark 11.1–11, see p. 90.

198

PROPER TWENTY-NINE
(Sunday closest to November 23)

First Lesson   Jeremiah 23.1–6

In our opening lesson **the Lord denounces the rulers who have so poorly shepherded the people Israel. God will gather the flock together and give them new shepherds, especially a just ruler in the line of David.** Jeremiah prophesied during the year that Babylon was conquering his country, and while Judah's last king Zedekiah (part of whose name meant *righteousness*) was ruling in Jerusalem. God would now have to act as shepherd to this people and will finally fulfill Israel's dream by raising up a wise and truly righteous ruler.

Psalm 46: The earth may be moved and kingdoms shaken, but God is our refuge. God is exalted among the nations of the earth.

Second Lesson (The Epistle)   Colossians 1.11–20

In this reading **Paul prays that the Colossians may be strengthened to meet whatever is to come, and he praises the Son as the visible likeness of the invisible God through whom all things were created. He is the head of his body, the church, and the source of its life.** There were some new disciples at Colossae who wished to worship Jesus as one of several lords. Paul insists that there can be no other divinities. God's full nature is in him. He is before all things and is the unifying principle for all created life. Through him we have been brought out of darkness into his kingdom, and by his sacrifice alone God reconciles all things.

The Gospel   Luke 23.35–43

In the Gospel **Jesus, as he hangs upon the cross, is mocked as the Christ and the King of the Jews. To a thief crucified with him he promises Paradise.** The story forces us also to ask, "What kind of ruler is this? What royal power does he have? What sort of God would allow God's chosen one to die like this?" Clearly the strength of God revealed in Christ is very different from the human understanding of kingship. Jesus' words to the thief are words of hope to all who die in every manner of circumstance.

For an alternative Gospel reading, Luke 19.29–38, see p. 227.

THE PRESENTATION
February 2

First Lesson   Malachi 3.1–4

In our Old Testament reading **the prophet promises that, as the day of the Lord's judgment nears, God's messenger will be sent to make ready the Lord's way.** The priests and temple servants, who say they are waiting for the Lord, need cleansing and purifying most of all. Suddenly the refiner will come to the temple, and then the offerings of the people will be pleasing to the Lord. On this day Christians recognize that, with the bringing of the child Jesus to the temple, the time of purifying judgment has begun.

Psalm 84 (or 84.1–6): A song of the pilgrims' happiness as they come to worship in the temple of the Lord.

Second Lesson (The Epistle)   Hebrews 2.14–18

In this lesson we learn how **Jesus has shared fully in all that it means to be human, and so is able to help us in our temptations.** Only by himself experiencing death could he break the power of death over us. Clearly this was not done for the benefit of angels (of which the author has just spoken) but for the human descendants of Abraham. Made of flesh and blood, participating in our sufferings and temptations, our brother Jesus becomes the merciful high priest so that our sins may be forgiven.

The Gospel   Luke 2.22–40

In our Gospel story **the infant Jesus is brought to the temple to be presented to the Lord in accordance with the law.** The time of Mary's purification is over, and the holy family comes to offer thanksgiving. Guided by the Spirit a devout man named Simeon perceives that this is the hoped for Messiah. In words which we have come to know as the *Nunc dimittis* ("Now let depart") Simeon foresees that this child will become the promised light to the Gentiles for the glory of Israel. But he also prophesies that Jesus will be a cause of division, sorrow and judgment. The ancient prophetess Anna then adds her testimony.

THE TRANSFIGURATION
August 6

First Lesson   Exodus 34.29–35

In our first reading we hear how **Moses' face glowed after he had spoken with the Lord.** When Moses came down from Mount Sinai after again receiving the ten commandments, the people were afraid to approach him because of the radiance of his face. Whenever he talked with the people, he had to wear a veil.

Psalm 99 (or 99.5–9): The holy and mighty Lord reigns on high. God spoke to Israel's leaders from a pillar of cloud and has forgiven them their misdeeds.

Second Lesson (The Epistle)   II Peter 1.13–21

The lesson presents **the apostle Peter, shortly before his death, as he calls to mind his vision of Jesus in majesty on the holy mountain and the heavenly voice which announced that this was God's beloved Son.** Peter was among those who were eyewitnesses to this revelation. It makes more sure the prophetic message which is like a lamp for us. But no one should make prophecy a matter solely of their own interpretation, for it has come through the Holy Spirit.

The Gospel   Luke 9.28–36

The Gospel is **the story of Jesus' transfiguration.** The narrative draws upon themes and symbols from Israel's past and its hopes for the future. Moses and Elijah represent the law and the prophets whose promises Jesus fulfills. While Jesus is praying, divine glory is reflected in his human person. Chosen disciples hear a voice from the cloud declaring that this is God's beloved Son.

ALL SAINTS DAY
November 1

First Lesson   Ecclesiasticus 44.1–10, 13–14

Our first lesson **sings the praises of famous individuals through whom God has been glorified.** Many different gifts have been theirs for the benefit of their descendants. Some persons of influence are rightly remembered for their worthy deeds, but others go unremembered. The passage serves as an introduction to chapters which honor specific heroes from Israel's past. It is part of a long section which praises the Lord for all God's marvelous works.

Psalm 149: A joyful song in which the faithful praise the Lord and anticipate the victory of justice.

Second Lesson (The Epistle)   Revelation 7.2–4, 9–17

This reading presents **a vision of those who have survived great tribulation and now worship before the throne of God and the Lamb.** An angel appears in order to save out of the tribes of Israel the true servants of God. Having been purified through their sufferings in association with the sacrifice of the Lamb, these myriad saints come from all over the world. Now the Lamb (which is a figure for Jesus) will be their shepherd, and they will suffer no longer.

The Gospel   Matthew 5.1–12

The Gospel is **the opening sayings of the Sermon on the Mount, words of both comfort and challenge.** The values of the reign of God are quite different from worldly standards. Those who are to find blessing will know want and thirst, if not because of their own circumstances, then for the sake of others. Those who hunger for righteousness will find fulfillment, but first they must suffer persecution.

ALL SAINTS DAY
November 1

First Lesson   Ecclesiasticus 2.7–11

This reading is **a counsel to trust in the Lord, remembering those in previous generations who put their faith in God.** The larger context shows that the author of this book recognized that the faithful were often tested and that they experienced many hardships. But there is also confidence that those who wait upon the Lord's mercy will never be disappointed.

Psalm 149: A joyful song in which the faithful praise the Lord and anticipate the victory of justice.

Second Lesson (The Epistle)   Ephesians 1.15–23

In this lesson **Paul gives thanks for the faith and love of the Ephesians, and extols the risen Christ who now reigns as head of the church.** The church is also the body of Christ and so experiences the fullness of its Lord. The apostle prays that these Christians may see with their inward eye the power of God who has raised and enthroned Jesus far above all earthly and heavenly dominions. How vast is the treasure that God offers to those who trust in God!

The Gospel   Luke 6.20–26

In our Gospel passage **Jesus pronounces blessings and woes, words of comfort and challenge, showing that the values of the reign of God are quite different from worldly standards.** Those who now are poor, hungry, sorrowful and persecuted will find their situation reversed, while the rich, satisfied and well spoken of will experience emptiness. Jesus' disciples must learn to share in material and spiritual deprivation in the world if they are to know the joy of the kingdom.

All three of these readings may be expanded as follows: Ecclesiasticus 2.1–11; Ephesians 1.11–23; Luke 6.20–36.

Alternative Lessons

FIRST SUNDAY OF ADVENT

Year B

Longer Gospel   Mark 13.24–37

In this Gospel lesson **Jesus presents his disciples with a vision of the end of human history and repeatedly urges them to be on watch.** The universe itself will reflect this transformation as the Son of Man comes. That time is near, but no one knows it exactly. Disciples must live expectantly and be on the alert for their Lord's coming.

THIRD SUNDAY OF ADVENT

Year B

Longer Second Lesson   I Thessalonians 5.12–28

As he concludes his letter to the church in Thessalonica, Paul exhorts the new converts to be at peace with one another and to live joyfully and prayerfully in readiness for the Lord's coming. Disciples are to care for each other, especially the weaker members, and never pay back wrong for wrong. Although they are to test what they hear, they are to be expectant to discover the Spirit in prophecy. Trusting in a faithful God, the followers of Jesus are to seek to avoid all forms of evil and to be made holy in every way.

Year C

Longer Second Lesson   Philippians 4.4–9

In this New Testament lesson **Paul invites the new disciples at Philippi joyously to exult in the Lord who is near at hand.** In prayer and thanksgiving they need have no anxiety. God's peace, which is beyond human understanding, will keep their hearts and thoughts in Jesus. They should fill their minds with all that is noble and loving, putting these things into practice as Paul has taught them to do. Even though Paul was experiencing his own troubles and may at this time have been in prison, this letter is often called "the epistle of joy."

HOLY NAME
January 1

Year A

Alternative Second Lesson   Philippians 2.9–13

In this lesson we learn that **after his resurrection the name that is above every name is Jesus. We confess him as Lord and are called to an obedient working out of our faith.** As this reading begins, Paul may well be repeating the words of an early Christian hymn. He goes on to tell the new disciples that they must work out their own salvation, while discovering that God is active in them for God's loving purpose.

SECOND SUNDAY AFTER CHRISTMAS

All Years

Alternative Gospel   Luke 2.41–52

Our Gospel tells **the story of Jesus' pilgrimage to Jerusalem as a young man of twelve, and the depths of his understanding in conversation with the teachers in the temple.** To his amazed and concerned parents, who had returned to Jerusalem after missing him on the journey homeward, Jesus responds that he must be in his Father's house. The narrative emphasizes Jesus' wisdom and comprehension of his Jewish heritage and points to his future role as a teacher whose authority will be greater than that of all the scribes and lawyers. When he returns to the temple late in his ministry, it will be to cleanse it before his rejection and death.

SECOND SUNDAY AFTER EPIPHANY

Year B

Longer First Lesson   I Samuel 3.1–20

In our Old Testament reading we hear how **Samuel learns that the Lord is calling him to make him God's prophet.** Three times the boy Samuel misunderstands and thinks that it is his mentor Eli summoning him during the night. Finally Eli realizes it must be the Lord, and tells Samuel to be ready. In the morning Samuel informs Eli of the punishment that is about to come upon his house. As Samuel grows, all Israel recognizes that he has been chosen by God to prophesy to the people.

FOURTH SUNDAY AFTER EPIPHANY

Year A

Longer Second Lesson   I Corinthians 1.18–31

In this reading **Paul directs the Corinthians' attention to God's way of using what is weak and lowly—even what the world regards as foolish—to accomplish God's purposes.** Paul emphasizes this understanding because a number of these new Christians had come to think of themselves as especially gifted and wise. Yet the cross has shown God active in the world in a manner surprising both to the Jews' expectation of powerful signs and to the Greeks' desire for worldly wisdom.

EIGHTH SUNDAY AFTER EPIPHANY

Year B

Longer Second Lesson   II Corinthians 3.4–11, 17–4.2

The law of Moses, Paul maintains, only brings death, and it is veiled to understanding unless seen from a Christian perspective. But, where the Spirit of the Lord is, life and liberty are experienced, and disciples are enabled to reflect the Lord's glory. Paul uses as an analogy the veil which Moses had to wear to mask the brightness of his face after talking with the Lord. The Spirit removes the need for such a veil. Entrusted with this commission, the apostle does not lose heart but conducts his ministry openly and honestly.

LAST SUNDAY AFTER EPIPHANY

Year B

Longer Second Lesson   II Peter 1.16–21

This lesson presents **the apostle Peter** as he **recalls his vision of Jesus in majesty on the holy mountain and the heavenly voice** which announced that this was God's beloved Son. Peter was among those who were eyewitnesses to this revelation. It makes more sure the prophetic message which is like a lamp for us. But no one should make this prophecy a matter solely of their own interpretation, for it has come through the Holy Spirit.

ASH WEDNESDAY

All Years

Alternative First Lesson   Isaiah 58.1–12

The Old Testament reading is **a denunciation of the injustices of those who only act at their religion. There is a promise of the Lord's favor for those who genuinely repent and care for the needy.** Fasts and many prayers are of no purpose and may be misused if they do not involve the liberation of the oppressed and help for the weak and afflicted. When there is justice and sharing, then the light of the Lord will rise out of the darkness and all the ruins will be rebuilt.

SECOND SUNDAY IN LENT

Year A

Longer Second Lesson   Romans 4.1–17

In this reading **Paul describes Abraham as a man who through faith found a right relationship with God. He is the father of all who trust in the Lord.** Paul uses the example of Abraham as a centerpiece in his argument that righteousness with God comes through faith and not by works of the law. The promise given to Abraham and his descendants was made beforehand and is independent of the outward sign of circumcision. King David also pronounces blessing on those who find righteousness apart from works.

Year C

Longer Gospel   Luke 13.22–35

Our Gospel tells of **Jesus' teaching on his way to Jerusalem and his determination to fulfill his prophetic destiny despite Herod's threat.** The reign of God cannot easily be entered. Some claim of earlier association with the Lord is no guarantee of acceptance. On the other hand, many from far away will find a place in the kingdom. Jesus then stresses his struggle against the forces of evil and illness and his expectation concerning what will happen to him in Jerusalem, the city that has killed so many prophets before him.

FOURTH SUNDAY IN LENT

Year A

Longer Second Lesson   Ephesians 5.1–14

In this New Testament lesson **disciples are called to walk in love and, as children of light, to avoid all the works of darkness.** Their present life is to be in sharp contrast with their actions before they became Christians. All that is done is to be exposed to the light. The passage closes with what was probably part of an ancient hymn used at baptisms.

Year C

Longer First Lesson   Joshua 4.19–24; 5.9–12

The Old Testament reading tells of **Israel's commemoration of its crossing over the Jordan River and the keeping of the first passover in the promised land.** Twelve stones used in the miraculous crossing of the river are set up as a reminder of God's mighty act and also to represent the twelve tribes of Israel. This happens at Gilgal, a name meaning *wheel,* which suggests the word-play as God declares the people's reproaches to be *rolled away.* Now that they can eat the produce of the countryside, there is no longer need for the miraculous manna of the wilderness.

MAUNDY THURSDAY

All Years

Longer Second Lesson   I Corinthians 11.23–32

In this reading **Paul recalls the tradition he received concerning the Lord's last supper and warns against eating the bread or drinking the cup unworthily.** The apostle reminds the Corinthians, who have shown an alarming tendency to divide up into factions, that this meal is a remembrance and reenactment of the Lord's offering of himself and forming of the new covenant. It proclaims the Lords' saving death and looks forward to his coming.

All Years

Alternative Gospel   Luke 22.14–30

Our Gospel is **the story of Jesus' last supper with his followers.** The sharing of the cup of wine and the bread is seen as an anticipation of the fulfillment of the kingdom of God. Jesus presents the broken bread as signifying his offering of himself. Even now the one who will betray the Son of Man is present among them. In response to a quarrel over which of the disciples should rank highest, Jesus offers them his example as their servant.

GOOD FRIDAY

All Years

Alternative First Lesson   Genesis 22.1–18

Our Old Testament reading is **the story of Abraham's willingness in obedience to the Lord's command to sacrifice his only son, Isaac, and the Lord's blessing of him.** The narrative illustrates Abraham's readiness to abandon all to serve the Lord. Originally it probably also was used as a model story encouraging the substitution of animal for human sacrifices. Ancient Israel was given a better understanding of God's will, and because of his obedience, Abraham received God's promise to him and his descendants.

All Years

Alternative First Lesson   Wisdom 2.1, 12–24

In this reading we hear how **deluded sinners plot to condemn the just individual. They do not understand God's plan or the hope of immortality.** These words were written in the century before the time of Christ, and the just person whom the unrighteous torment is probably an idealization of the good and faithful Jew. He is called God's son because he reflects the character of God as his Father. Christians see in his goodness, sufferings and the promise of his immortality a prefigurement of Jesus.

EASTER DAY
Principal Service

Year A

Longer Gospel   John 20.1–18

Our Gospel tells of **the discovery of the empty tomb and Jesus' appearance to Mary Magdalene.** While it is still dark, Mary comes and finds that the stone used to cover the tomb has been moved away. She runs and brings Peter and another disciple whom Jesus loved. Although no human eye catches sight of Jesus' rising from death, these first witnesses see the discarded grave wrappings and the other disciple perceives and believes. Mary remains weeping at the graveside and talks with a man she assumes to be the gardener. He speaks her name, and she knows her Lord.

SECOND SUNDAY OF EASTER

Year A

Alternative First Lesson   Genesis 8.6–16, 9.8–16

The Old Testament reading is the **conclusion of the story of the flood. It tells of God's promise to Noah and to future generations never again to drown the whole earth.** God establishes the covenant with a sign—the rainbow that is seen in the storm clouds. The covenant is made with the whole of creation. At the beginning of new life it signifies God's purpose to preserve and save the world, not to destroy it.

Year B

Alternative First Lesson   Isaiah 26.2–9, 19

Our reading from the Old Testament is **a poem expressing trust in the Lord who guides in the way of righteousness and who will raise the dead to life.** God brings low the lofty and wins the victory for the poor and oppressed. Those who trust in the Lord are kept in peace. They will know new life.

Year C

Alternative First Lesson   Job 42.1–6

In this Old Testament lesson **Job, who had demanded justice for his own life and was then encountered by the living and awesome God, now responds in great humility.** Job recalls some of the earlier words of the Lord and realizes how far he has been from any true understanding. God is powerful beyond all measure. Having been confronted by God, Job utterly repents.

Year C

Longer Second Lesson   Revelation 1.1–19

This reading is **the beginning of the Revelation made known to a disciple named John: a series of visions which opens with an appearance of the risen and resplendent Lord.** The seer is on an island, sent there by God or perhaps banished because of persecution, and is commanded to record his visions to send to seven churches. Jesus is seen in mystic glory and described like the divine figure who had appeared earlier in a dream to the prophet Daniel. Having died and returned to life Jesus holds power over death and hell.

THIRD SUNDAY OF EASTER

Year A

Alternative First Lesson   Isaiah 43.1–12

In this Old Testament reading **the Lord assures Israel that they are God's chosen people. They are not to fear; God will save them.** It is the time of the end of the exile, and God, who created the servant Israel, now promises to deliver the Lord's own out of all their troubles. They are to be God's witnesses to the nations, the Lord's testimony that there is no other God.

Year B

Alternative First Lesson   Micah 4.1–5

In our Old Testament reading **the prophet presents his vision of the time when Jerusalem will become a spiritual capital for the world.** Mount Zion shall be raised up so that the Lord's teaching

211

will be a source of wisdom for many peoples. Never again will there be war. Nations will show great toleration for each other's worship as Israel continues faithful to its God.

Year C

Alternative First Lesson   Jeremiah 32.36–41

In this lesson from the Old Testament **the prophet Jeremiah is given the promise of a time of deliverance and of a new relationship between God and the people.** It has been Jeremiah's heavy burden to prophesy the destruction of Jerusalem and the exile of the people to Babylon. But now he learns that the Lord's wrath will one day end. God will restore the people and, as their God, make an everlasting covenant with them.

FOURTH SUNDAY OF EASTER

Year A

Alternative First Lesson   Nehemiah 9.6–15

In our Old Testament lesson **Ezra, the scribe, remembers the Lord's creative acts by which Israel was made the people of God.** The time is the period after the exile. Jerusalem has been rebuilt and the covenant renewed. Ezra has called for a day of fasting and now praises the Lord who has fulfilled the divine promises. God gave the people the commandments and brought them safely through the wilderness to this land.

Year B

Longer First Lesson   Acts 4.23–37

In this reading we hear **Peter and John pray that they may continue to preach and to heal in Jesus' name. The early community is filled with the Holy Spirit and with care for one another.** The two apostles have just been warned by the religious officials not to teach about Jesus. But God is with them against earthly authorities. Greed and anxiety with regard to material possessions are overcome by grace. The author of Acts may present a somewhat idyllic picture, but there is no denying the power of the gospel to bring disciples to a profoundly new way of life.

Year B

Alternative First Lesson   Ezekiel 34.1–10

Our Old Testament reading is **a sharp prophecy against those
who are meant to be shepherds of the people but who instead
neglect the sheep and care only for themselves.** The temptation is
always strong for leaders to avoid tasks of mercy and to seek personal benefit from the ones they are called to serve. As the exile
draws to an end, the Lord tells Ezekiel to denounce the leaders of
Israel who feed off the sheep they are assigned to feed.

Year C

Alternative First Lesson   Numbers 27.12–23

In this lesson from the Old Testament we hear how **Joshua is chosen to succeed Moses as the leader and shepherd of the people Israel.** The people are about to end their long journey out of slavery
in Egypt through the wilderness to the promised land. Moses will
be unable to enter the new land with them but, before he dies, he
passes his God-given authority on to Joshua.

FIFTH SUNDAY OF EASTER

Year A

Alternative First Lesson   Deuteronomy 6.20–25

The Old Testament reading passes on **the tradition concerning
the significance of the commandments which the Lord gave to Israel after they had been brought out of Egypt.** It is probable that
these words come from an ancient Jewish passover liturgy. They tell
how Israel became the people of the Lord and were given their heritage. For their own good and in response to God's election they
have the commandments to obey.

Year B

Alternative First Lesson   Deuteronomy 4.32–40

In our Old Testament lesson **Moses reminds the people of all that
God has done for them and charges them to obey God's commandments.** The passage stresses God's uniqueness and the very special
and intimate relationship God has chosen with Israel. God has

213

revealed God's divine person to them, saved and loved them, and given them their heritage. They, in turn, are meant to be a disciplined people who respond by keeping God's statutes.

Year B

Longer Second Lesson   I John 3.14–24

In this passage we learn that **Christian faith expresses itself in active love. Hatred leads to death, but those who love have crossed over from death to life.** Jesus has given us an example, and by putting our trust in him and caring for one another we can know an intimacy with God which will be confirmed by the Holy Spirit. If we seek to live by love, we may rest assured that God is well able to overcome our guilt.

SIXTH SUNDAY OF EASTER

Year A

Alternative First Lesson   Isaiah 41.17–20

In this Old Testament lesson **the Lord promises the people Israel that they will be cared for even in the wilderness.** There will be water for them in barren lands, and trees will grow. So does the prophet foresee the people returning safely home after the exile. By leading them through the desert, the Lord will show all the world who alone is the true God.

Year B

Alternative First Lesson   Isaiah 45.11–13, 18–19

In the first lesson we hear **the Lord's response to those who would question God for choosing Cyrus, King of Persia, as the divine agent to bring the exiled people of Judah home to Jerusalem.** God may sometimes seem to work in mysterious ways, but the Lord is the creator of heaven and earth. Not just Israel but all people and all history are under God's rule.

Year C

Alternative First Lesson   Joel 2.21–27

In our Old Testament reading **the prophet pictures a time of great abundance and gladness.** All plague and famine are in the past. The Lord will be present to the people of God, and they will never again be put to shame.

ASCENSION DAY

Year B

Alternative First Lesson   Ezekiel 1.3–5a, 15–22, 26–28

The book of the prophet Ezekiel begins with **a dramatic vision of the heavenly throne-chariot and of the majesty of the glory of the Lord.** The impressive imagery conveys a sense of the divine transcendence and the incomprehensible power of God to move at will and to know all things. These are important themes for the prophet, and on this day they suggest to Christians the grandeur of their risen Lord.

Year C

Alternative First Lesson   II Kings 2.1–15

The Old Testament reading is **the story of the taking up of the prophet Elijah into heaven and the passing on of his power to Elisha.** The narrative illustrates the great favor Elijah found in the eyes of the Lord, as he is carried away in a chariot of fire. Elisha is in despair, but God does not leave the people without new prophetic vision. On this day Christians perceive in the story allusions to the ascension of Jesus and the promise of the coming of the Holy Spirit.

All Years

Alternative Gospel   Mark 16.9–15, 19–20

Our Gospel lesson presents **a summary of appearances of the risen Lord. He was taken up into heaven after commissioning his disciples to preach the gospel to the whole of creation.** The passage was apparently not part of Mark's original Gospel and draws upon stories told more fully in the other Gospels. It effectively relates the themes of Jesus' resurrection and ascension with the missionary activity of the early church.

SEVENTH SUNDAY OF EASTER

Year A

Longer First Lesson   Acts 1.1–14

In the opening passage of the Acts of the Apostles the author presents **a summary of the last events of Jesus' ministry on earth and his instructions before he is envisioned being lifted up into heaven.** This book is formally dedicated to Theophilus who may have been an early convert to Christianity. The missionary work of the church will spread outward from Jerusalem. In obedience to their Lord's command, the disciples now return to the city and prayerfully await their empowering baptism with the Holy Spirit.

Alternative First Lesson   Ezekiel 39.21–29

In this lesson **the prophet foretells that the Lord's glory and judgment will be known to all nations. Although Israel has been handed over to exile because of iniquity, God's people will be brought back to their own land.** The exile was just because of Israel's sins, but now they will learn the depths of God's mercy. God will not be hidden from them, and in their new life God will pour out the Spirit upon the people.

Year B

Alternative First Lesson   Exodus 28.1–4, 9–10, 29–30

In our Old Testament reading **Moses receives instructions regarding the priestly garments and other articles to be worn by Aaron and his sons.** These special vestments signify the priest's sacred role. On the ephod, or apron-like garment, the names of the twelve tribes are represented. In the attached breast-piece are kept the Urim and Thummin, two objects used to determine the Lord's will. The reading of the lesson on this day is meant to allude to Jesus in his role as the eternal high priest.

216

Alternative First Lesson   I Samuel 12.19–24

In this lesson **the people request Samuel's petitions for their for-giveness because they have desired a king to be their ruler. Samuel promises his continual prayers and that all will be well if they will worship the Lord faithfully.** The discussion indicates a great division among the people in Israel. Some wanted a royal form of government to help them fight against their enemies. Others feared that this kind of earthly rule would lead away from the understanding that God alone was the true ruler of their lives. On this day the reading is used to cause Christians to reflect on the awareness that the ascended Jesus is their king.

THE DAY OF PENTECOST

Year A

Alternative First Lesson   Ezekiel 11.17–20

In our Old Testament lesson **the Lord promises a new day for Israel, and a new Spirit in their hearts, so that they may truly become God's people.** In the Lord's name the prophet foresees an end to the exile in foreign nations. The people will return home, forsaking all form of idolatry. With Spirit-filled hearts of flesh they will obey and know their God.

Year B

Alternative First Lesson   Isaiah 44.1–8

In the Old Testament lesson **God promises to pour out the Spirit upon the people as water is poured forth on thirsty ground.** The time of the exile is over. God's servant people, Jacob—God's chosen Israel—will be blessed and will flourish. The Lord has foretold all this, and there is no other God.

Year C

Alternative First Lesson   Joel 2.28–32

In the opening lesson **the prophet foresees a day when the Lord will pour forth the Spirit on all peoples creating prophecies, dreams and visions.** There will be signs in the natural world as well, on earth and in the sky, for this will be a time of great transformation—a day of judgment as well as opportunity for salvation. Christians used this oracle to help signify the meaning of the Pentecost experience.

Alternative Gospel   John 14.8–17

In our Gospel **Jesus tells his disciples that in him the Father has been revealed, and he promises the gift of another Counselor, the Spirit of truth, to be with them.** The Lord is speaking with his followers on the night before his death. Soon he will be taken away from them, but all that they ask the Father will now grant in Jesus' name. As they continue to love Jesus and keep his commands, they will realize the indwelling Spirit who will take Jesus' place in their midst.

TRINITY SUNDAY

Year C

Longer Gospel   John 16.5–15

In our Gospel **Jesus tells his disciples that his going away will mean the coming of the Holy Spirit who will guide them into all truth.** The Counselor-Spirit will bring true judgment into the world. Everything declared by the Spirit will be received from Jesus, even as all which the Father has belongs to Jesus. The Spirit, then, reveals Jesus who himself has made the Father known.

PROPER FIVE

Year B

Longer First Lesson   Genesis 3.1–21

In our Old Testament story we hear of **Adam and Eve's act of disobedience in the Garden of Eden and its results for the human race.** The narrative is richly woven with themes meant to help explain harsh features of the human condition: from pain, hard labor and death, to feelings of shame about sexuality—from fear of God to estrangement from the creatures of the earth, symbolized by the serpent. By their disobedience and coming to the knowledge of good and evil the man and woman now live in disharmony with the world and even with one another.

PROPER SIX

Year A

Longer Gospel   Matthew 9.35–10.15

In our Gospel reading **Jesus continues his mission of preaching, teaching and healing, and he commissions his twelve disciples in this ministry with him.** The need for this work is great. The twelve are constituted as a kind of new Israel, and their healing acts and proclamation tell that God's healing power has drawn near. For the time being this ministry is to be concentrated on the Jewish people. The missionaries are to travel about trusting that they will be given what they need, and they are to accept welcome or rejection as it comes.

PROPER SEVEN

Year A

Longer Gospel   Matthew 10.16–33

In our Gospel **Jesus warns his disciples of troubles to come, but offers them the assurance of the Father's care and his own readiness to support them before God as they speak up for him.** Because they are Jesus' disciples, people will do to them what they did to him. There will be persecution and divided families. But soon the divine judge, the Son of Man, will come. Disciples are not to be afraid. The Spirit of the Father will be with them. The body may be destroyed, but not the soul which trusts in God.

Year B

Longer Gospel   Mark 4.35–5.20

The Gospel lesson is **the stories of the stilling of the storm and the exorcism and healing of the Gerasene demoniac.** The two narratives were used by the early churches to illustrate the majesty of the Lord Jesus who had power to control both natural forces and the inner ragings of the mind. Symbolically the stories reveal him to be sovereign over cosmic evil. Audiences of the time would recognize the parallel between Jesus' lordship over the storm and the power of God shown when God, according to myth, conquered over the watery chaos monster and formed the world.

PROPER NINE

Year C

Longer Second Lesson   Galatians 6.1–18

In this lesson **Paul closes his letter to the Galatians with an appeal that they bear their own responsibilities and help one another, while remembering that nothing counts in comparison with the glory of Christ's saving cross.** Each should do all he can to sow for a spiritual harvest. These new disciples are not to make the mistake of thinking that salvation is influenced either by circumcision or uncircumcision. The power of the cross has formed something new, an Israel to which both Jews and Gentiles belong. Paul's own experiences as an apostle have left him with signs of a suffering like that of Jesus.

PROPER ELEVEN

Year C

Longer First Lesson   Genesis 18.1–14

In our Old Testament story **the Lord appears to Abraham and promises that he and Sarah will have a son.** As often in Old Testament narratives, the Lord's presence is disguised, this time in one of three visitors. Abraham may suspect God's nearness, but he also generously fulfills his duty of hospitality to strangers. Because both of them are well beyond the years of childbearing, Sarah laughs when she overhears the promise. Yet Abraham will place his trust in God's power and through this son become the father of a great people.

PROPER THIRTEEN

Year C

Longer First Lesson   Ecclesiastes 1.12–14; 2.1–67, 11, 18–23

In our opening reading **the Teacher reflects on the useless character of life and the fact that the fruit of all our labors will be inherited by others.** The author (who fictionally is King Solomon) refers to himself as Qoheleth, which is variously translated as Teacher, Preacher or Philosopher. His view of human existence is pessimistic. All pleasures and riches are a chasing after the wind, and God's ways are unknown. It is one of the Bible's remarkable features that it includes this very human attitude together with its other views which indicate God's purposes for life.

Longer Second Lesson   Colossians 3.5–17

In this New Testament lesson **disciples are urged to put off their former vices and to clothe themselves with Christian virtues, doing everything in the name of the Lord Jesus.** This is the language of a homily about the meaning of baptism. As God's chosen people, Christians are members of one body in which barriers of race, religion and class are overcome. Forgiven, they are to forgive, teaching one another in wisdom and singing songs of thanksgiving, while all is bound together in love.

PROPER FOURTEEN

Year B

Longer Second Lesson   Ephesians 4.25–5.2

In this lesson **Christians are urged to conform to a new way of life which is pleasing to the Holy Spirit. They are to have a love like the love of Christ.** All manner of evil is to be shunned. Especially are the new converts to put away spitefulness and other sins which harm the one body and grieve the Spirit with which they have been sealed in baptism. The model is none other than God as God is revealed in the Christ who sacrificed himself for us.

PROPER FIFTEEN

Year A

Longer First Lesson   Isaiah 56.1–7

In our opening lesson **the Lord exhorts the people to do what is just because the time of righteous salvation is close at hand. The temple will be a house of prayer for all nations.** Even eunuchs will not be excluded and will find an everlasting name. This vision of hope emphasizes the outgoing aspects of Israel's faith. Historically it deals with the fact that after the exile certain non-Israelites had come to live in Jerusalem and serve in the temple. The passage sets the conditions for their participation, but also looks beyond to a day when many peoples will worship the God of Israel.

PROPER SEVENTEEN

Year C

Longer First Lesson   Ecclesiasticus 10.7–18

Our opening lesson is **a condemnation of human pride, which reminds of human frailty, and instructs that the Lord pulls down the mighty and puts the humble in their place.** The root of such pride is the sin of a human refusal to recognize dependence on God. Individuals, especially rulers, and nations which are arrogant will be brought to destruction. Every mortal will end in death from which not even the doctor's skill can save him.

PROPER TWENTY

Year B

Longer First Lesson   Wisdom 1.16–2.1, 6–22

The first reading describes **the philosophy of deluded sinners who, finding no purpose in life, think only of their own enjoyment and persecute the righteous.** They not only wish to take advantage of the good man, but want also to test him and finally to put him to death because his very goodness is a reproach to their way of life. They will make trial both of the one who sees himself as God's son and the God who he believes will protect him. Blinded by their wickedness, they perceive neither God's purposes nor God's rewards for the blameless. Christians have seen in these words a foreshadowing of Christ's sufferings and vindication.

Year C

Longer First Lesson   Amos 8.4–12

The first lesson is **a judgment on social injustice and religious hypocrisy.** On celebrations like the New Moon and Sabbaths no work was allowed. Yet traders were so full of greed that they only mechanically observed the festivals and could not wait for them to be over so that they might again swindle the poor. Such offences are also sins against the Lord. There will be earthquake, flood and the sun's eclipse. The feasts will become times of mourning, and no one will be able to find the word of the Lord.

PROPER TWENTY-ONE

Year B

Longer Second Lesson   James 4.7–5.6

This lesson offers **a series of counsels and warnings: Christians are to draw near to the Lord in penitence, not presuming to judge their neighbors, and knowing the great dangers of riches and wealth's exploitation of others.** If disciples will stand up to the devil with his temptations, he will go away. God will then come close as we come near to God. While our condition of sin must lead to mourning, God raises us up. Those who criticize and judge their neighbors put themselves in God's place. Always we must recognize that whatever we frail mortals do or plan can only be accomplished by the Lord's will.

PROPER TWENTY-TWO

Year B

Longer Second Lesson   Hebrews 2.1–18

In this lesson we learn **how carefully we must heed the message that the Lord has delivered and confirmed for us. Jesus has now shared in human life and, as our leader and high priest, is able to help us in our temptations.** Only by himself experiencing death could he break the power of death over us. Clearly this was not done for angels but for the human descendants of Abraham. Made of flesh and blood, participating in our sufferings and temptations, our brother Jesus has become the perfect and merciful high priest so that our sins may be forgiven.

Year C

Longer First Lesson   Habakkuk 1.1–13; 2.1–4

In our opening reading **the prophet bitterly complains to the Lord about the injustice and violence in the world. God answers that justice will come in time; meanwhile the righteous will live by faithfulness and loyalty.** It is the time of the Chaldean (or Babylonian) invasion. Their mighty armies sweep everything before them. Habakkuk cannot understand how God can allow all this evil and destruction. He takes his position in the watchtower to await the Lord's reply. Those who are right with God will continue to live by their trust.

Longer Second Lesson   II Timothy 1.1–14

This passage is **the opening of Paul's letter to Timothy. He calls upon his friend and coworker to remain strong in his vocation in Christ and to guard the truth which has been entrusted to him.** He is to keep alive the flame of God's gift of the Spirit and to make his testimony without shame. Together with Paul he must recognize that suffering is a part of his calling. It is not we ourselves but Christ Jesus who has made this ministry possible, for he has broken death's power and brought life and immortality to light.

PROPER TWENTY-THREE

Year B

Longer Gospel   Mark 10.17–31

In the Gospel **Jesus counsels a would-be disciple to sell all for the benefit of the poor and follow him, and he then teaches how hard it is for those with riches to enter the kingdom. Disciples who now surrender much will receive back all manner of new relationships in the age to come.** Jesus first refuses to let himself be called *good* since that description belongs to God alone. He then finds that the man has tried to live out his duties toward his neighbors in response to divine love. But the decision for discipleship must go beyond this. If the heart is divided by desires for worldly security, there is no way one can enter into the kingdom's loving justice. Yet by the power of God people can be converted and saved.

Year C

Longer Second Lesson   II Timothy 2.3–15

In this reading **Paul bids Timothy to be a faithful worker, reminding himself and others of Jesus' resurrection and of the new
life that is to be known with him.** Although Paul is shut up in prison,
the gospel is free in the world. The apostle reflects on his tribula-
tions and encourages his younger associate to accept his share of sufferings and to serve like a good soldier, a disciplined athlete or a
hard-working farmer. Especially should he warn his people to avoid
disputes over words. The verses which begin "If we died with him,
we shall live with him" seem part of an early Christian hymn.

PROPER TWENTY-FIVE

Year B

Longer First Lesson   Isaiah 59.1–4, 9–19

In the Old Testament lesson **the prophet denounces the sin of the
people and they lament; there is no righteousness in the land; injustice is everywhere. Soon the Lord will come as a mighty warrior
to bring retribution.** Darkness reigns over the nation and sin multiplies. Truth goes unspoken. Sin has formed a barrier between God
and the people. But the Lord is putting on the armor of righteousness. All will learn to fear God.

PROPER TWENTY-SIX

Year C

Longer Second Lesson   II Thessalonians 1.1–12

In this lesson **Paul greets the new disciples in Thessalonica and
gives thanks for the increase of their faith under persecution. God
will repay those who afflict them and do not obey the gospel.** When
the Lord is revealed, all accounts will be balanced. Paul suggests
that the Thessalonians' present troubles may be a way of proving
them worthy of the kingdom. He is so proud of their growing faith
and love that he boasts about them to others. He offers them his
prayers.

PROPER TWENTY-SEVEN

Year C

Longer Gospel   Luke 20.27–38

In the Gospel **the Sadducees ask a question about the legal status after the resurrection of a woman who had been married to a succession of brothers. Jesus replies that resurrection means a different existence from earthly life and that it depends on a God who has a personal and living relationship with all people.** The Sadducees did not believe in resurrection from death, and they attempted to make the idea seem absurd by posing this question based on the law's requirement that a man should marry his brother's childless widow. Jesus cuts through their apparent cleverness. There is no need for marriage after the resurrection. What is more, the Bible continues to speak of the patriarchs as though they were still alive before God. In this Jesus perceives a profound truth about God's unfailing care.

PROPER TWENTY-EIGHT

Year B

Longer First Lesson   Daniel 12.1–4a, 5–13

In our Old Testament lesson **Daniel is given a vision of the end of human history: after a period of great distress, some will be brought to their salvation and others to eternal disgrace.** This was a time of persecution for Israel which took place two centuries before the life of Christ. The "abomination of desolation" refers to a desecrating statue which the Syrian emperor set up in the Jerusalem temple. But this is an oracle of hope which makes use of the veiled language and imagery common to apocalyptic visions. Evil will mount up to a last desperate effort before Michael, Israel's patron angel, intervenes to bring justice. In what is a new idea for Judaism, even the faithful dead will be raised to receive their reward.

PROPER TWENTY-NINE

Year C

Alternative Gospel   Luke 19.29–38

In this Gospel lesson **Jesus, his long journey over, approaches the holy city of Jerusalem, while his disciples hail him as the king who comes in the Lord's name.** He has a colt brought to him and, as did the royal figures of old, Jesus rides on it while his many followers spread their garments in the way and shout praises to God. Here is great drama as the Lord comes to the city he would save, but also acute irony for those who know what lies ahead.

Index of Biblical Readings

228

Index of Biblical Readings

230

Index of Biblical Readings